Praise for

"In *WorkParty*, Jaclyn Johnson generously shares the secrets to her success: be nice, take risks, and work your butt off. Whether you're looking to turn your side hustle into your main gig or thrive in your corporate job, this is the book you need to take your career to the next level—on your own terms."

—Refinery29

"*WorkParty* hilariously and oftentimes heartbreakingly captures the real struggles of being a risk-taking woman in the modern world. It's a much-needed combo of real talk, confessions, and lessons learned along the way—it's sure to leave you ready to tackle, or give a middle finger, to any obstacle in your way."

—Chelsea Handler

"*WorkParty* is a must-read for any woman looking to cultivate her passion, build her business, and create the life she has always wanted, on her own terms."

—Rebecca Minkoff

HOW TO CREATE & CULTIVATE
THE CAREER OF YOUR DREAMS

Jaclyn Johnson

Illustrations by Chloe White

GALLERY BOOKS

New York   London   Toronto   Sydney   New Delhi

G

Gallery Books
An Imprint of Simon & Schuster, Inc.
1230 Avenue of the Americas
New York, NY 10020

First Gallery Books trade paperback edition March 2019

GALLERY BOOKS and colophon are registered trademarks of Simon & Schuster, Inc.

For information about special discounts for bulk purchases,
please contact Simon & Schuster Special Sales at 1-866-506-1949
or business@simonandschuster.com.

The Simon & Schuster Speakers Bureau can bring authors to your live event. For more information or to book an event, contact the Simon & Schuster Speakers Bureau at 1-866-248-3049 or visit our website at www.simonspeakers.com.

All illustrations courtesy of Chloe White
Interior design by Davina Mock-Maniscalco

Manufactured in the United States of America

10   9   8   7   6   5   4   3   2

Library of Congress Cataloging-in-Publication Data

Names: Johnson, Jaclyn, author.
Title: WorkParty : how to create & cultivate the career of your dreams /
   Jaclyn Johnson.
Other titles: Work party
Description: New York : Gallery Books, 2018.
Identifiers: LCCN 2018014251| ISBN 9781501190834 (hardback) | ISBN
   9781501190841 (trade paper) | ISBN 9781501190858 (ebook)
Subjects: LCSH: Women—Employment—United States. | Sex discrimination
   against women—United States. | Businesswomen—United States. | Success in
   business—United States. | Job satisfaction. | BISAC: BUSINESS & ECONOMICS
   / Entrepreneurship.
Classification: LCC HD6095 .J64 2018 | DDC 650.1—dc23
LC record available at https://lccn.loc.gov/2018014251

ISBN 978-1-5011-9083-4
ISBN 978-1-5011-9084-1 (pbk)
ISBN 978-1-5011-9085-8 (ebook)

For JoAnn, my unofficial cofounder,
my sometimes accountant, but always my mother.
I love you.

And to Arianna Schioldager and Dana Kelly,
who helped me turn the last eleven years of my life
into 62,899 words. Eternally grateful to you
for joining me on this wild ride.

contents

introduction

Hard work = the American Dream. This is what I was raised on.

WorkParty = the new American Dream. Or, rather, that's what I'm proposing. What I mean is: WorkParty is the hard work that the American dream is based on, but driven by passion rather than necessity. When you're workpartying, you don't clock in or out, but tune into every minute because you are a part of something you love.

And it's unbelievably hard.

As a young professional in my twenties, I suffered two massive blows. I looked, leapt, moved across the country for a job, and then I was abruptly let go. Attempting to turn that door into a window, I launched a promising company with a trusted business partner, but soon discovered that she had made some detrimental decisions for the company without my knowledge. I went through a brutal business breakup. I was twenty-four.

But it was worthwhile—by the time I was thirty-two, I had sold a company, launched a much-buzzed-about new one, bought my first home, found the love of my life, and had a million ups and downs in between.

How?

By turning distrust into determination, frustration into fuel, and heartache into hard work.

Oh yeah, and that determination, fuel, and hard work? It can be so. much. fun.

Not because my office is filled with streamers and champagne. Hardly. It's spreadsheets and team meetings, where I happen to be surrounded by other strong women. Together, we're all creating and cultivating the careers of our dreams together. We leaned in, and now we are standing up. We are redefining work for a new generation of women who want it all and more, and guess what? They can have it and so can you.

I am not the Wolf of Wall Street; I am not Tony Robbins here to espouse my great theories on life; this is not a marketing scheme. Rather, *WorkParty* is the lessons I learned and the advice I wish I'd gotten when I was twenty-one and at my first major job. Or when I was twenty-four, bright-eyed and a bit naïve, launching my first company with a business partner. Or twenty-eight and striking out on my own. Or even thirty, having created and cultivated a community of over five hundred thousand women.

So consider this my official invitation to you to start your own #workparty. Where creative and entrepreneurial women celebrate each other's successes. Where you can celebrate your own achievements because you are doing it all yourself, unabashedly, at the best bash the workplace has ever known. Because, listen, the joy has been sucked out of our careers for far too long. And we're bringing it back. Who said business had to be boring?

These are my experiences, these are the hard-fought lessons I learned, and this is your guide to making it all happen and more.

Work hard. Party on.

chapter one

When Crushing It Crushes You

You aren't good or bad at anything you haven't tried. You can't fear what you haven't figured out yet, and sometimes naïveté can be the best business strategy of all.

But sometimes you might try something, give it your all, even move across the country for it, and get fired. Or, *ahem,* "politely let go."

That's the beginning of my story, at least, but let's back up a little bit.

I started my career during a time I like to call "P.E."

Pre-exclamation. Pre-emoji. There was no such thing as a hashtag either.

No one was livestreaming their lives, outfits, or meals. And I truly believed life was somewhat like a rom-com: work hard, move to the big city, a dashing dude sweeps you off your feet, and you live happily ever after in your apartment that is always spotless, right? Wrong.

But there I was, a recent graduate of NYU, and like so many other women who trekked the sidewalks of Manhattan in heels before me (before you realize you need to bring flats with you everywhere because, again, #notlikeamovie), I was eager to crush it at my career.

The big-corner-office, chic-power-suit, boss-haircut, eager-assistant, town-car kind of crushing it. And for a minute, it was working. I dyed my hair black and spent a critical few minutes every day blow-drying my side-swooping bangs. Think big belts and boho bags. Sure, I was dating a club promoter—not exactly the sort of partner who shared my corner-office goals, no, but he did facilitate some wild nights that ended with sunrises and pizza slices.

I had happened into a career in a little something called "social media" five years before it would hit the mainstream. I was a boss at Blogspot, I was tweeting on Twitter, I was posting in forums (I know, #LOL), and I had a blog, which I know sounds not-that-exciting present day, but at the time was a rare thing. I called the blog Some Notes on Napkin (SNON), and it was my own little corner of the internet, my musings on twenty-something life in the Big Apple with a bent on fashion and style.

The first post, April 7, 2007, is still up (go ahead and Google it) and is called "Leave It to Karl [Lagerfeld]." SNON was a mix of cutout editorial collages I put together in PowerPoint, trends I was loving, places to eat, my literal LiveJournal of my twenties. I posted playlists, outfit inspirations, outfit flat lays, art, design, and street style. Less a digital diary than an archive of inspiration, trends, and makers I had my eye on, and people were reading it. A lot of people.

I didn't even know what analytics were until a colleague showed me and said, "You get about three thousand people to your site every day." UM, WHAT? Who? It wasn't just my mom? What was this thing I had created? Now, many years later, there is a part of me that is embarrassed looking back at an internet time machine, a relic of a former life, but back then, I was Carrie Bradshaw–ing my life in NYC with my friends, living alone in the East Village in a five-story walk-up, and somehow making it work before blogging equaled major dollars. The internet was a truly authentic and vulnerable place.

Now I want to note that at the time my blog made approximately zero dollars. So I spent my days running accounts at a startup marketing agency by the name of Attention, now a preeminent global communications firm with household-name clients. Back then, though, I was employee number three in a company full of all dudes and was brought on to spearhead their "pink vertical," and by that I mean their fashion and beauty clients. I had quite literally responded to a Craigslist job posting that read "Seeking Female Account Executive Interested in Fashion and the Internet." I immediately responded to the flagrantly non-politically-correct ad, and the rest, as they say, was history.

Despite Attention's office space—a.k.a. the back of an under-construction corner in someone else's office in the Flatiron district—the agency was actually really ahead of its time. Sure, the front office was being run by an online poker company that bore a *Boiler Room* resemblance. Spoiler alert: They were raided by the FBI about three months into our office cohabitation. But we kept our (much more legal) business chugging along. Attention's services were dubbed "word-of-mouth marketing," the beginnings of what would become social media marketing before it had a name. Social media as we know and heart it today wasn't really a thing, which means there was no snap, tag, or share yet. But there was Twitter, Facebook, blogging, and forums—all things I was familiar with and good at.

I had stumbled upon the whitespace (more on that later) in the newfound digital marketing world, and I understood the internet in the way forty-something white men couldn't (and still can't). Because of that savvy, I was getting promoted, poached, and escalated up the corporate ladder so quickly that I assumed that the next stop was #towncarlife.

It all came naturally to me, this new digital language and world. I vividly remember high school English class always being a struggle (shout out, Mrs. Pilcher). The problem? My writing style. I wrote in short, quippy, and to-the-point sentences—meaning no "hereafters" or "therefores." Conversational and relatable, my writing wasn't exactly the five-paragraph structure my English teacher wanted. The papers I wrote were marked up in red, citing poor syntax and too many colloquialisms. And yet I couldn't understand what I was doing wrong. Only after graduating magna cum laude with a journalism degree from New York University did I realize what I had been doing.

I had been blogging my way through high school English.

I was talking in tweets before Twitter existed. Beginning, middle, and end? Supporting paragraphs and conclusions? No thanks. You can keep your MLA format and debate the AP style guide. At Attention and on Some Notes on Napkins, I was finally putting that impulse to good use.

pause

Keep in mind: If you want to succeed, you have to be able to break from tradition fearlessly and sometimes recklessly and sometimes while feeling genuinely uncomfortable with everyone telling you no. No truly successful entrepreneur these days has followed some preordained path to success. There is no "right." There's only saying yes, figuring it out, and knowing there will be a few bumps along the way.

For the first time in my semiadult life, I had found my niche. And when I wasn't updating my now thriving blog, I was grinding it out creating some of the first social media campaigns. At my day job, I launched the Barbie x MAC collaboration, was seeding Estée Lauder products to influential tastemakers before they were called influencers or tastemakers, and was creating Facebook pages for brands and building content strategies, essentially establishing protocol of how this whole online world could work. AND I LOVED IT.

Influencers, if you don't already know, (mainly) started as bloggers—the girls taking outfit of the day (#OOTD) photos, DIYers, and the like—who turned their blogs into bona fide businesses (more on that later!).

And about five months into my tenure as the sole female employee at Attention, two more women were hired. I rapidly on-boarded them as my ride-or-die best friends, and I'm proud to say they are still my number ones. They affected my career in countless ways (more on that later, too!), and I am forever grateful for our time spent in that cramped office space, rats and all.

We—the influencers—had immediately seen the potential in this digital world. And because I understood the world from both the blogging end and the marketing end, I knew I was capable. I was working both sides of the table, and as such, I brought ideas to that table.

To his credit, my boss at Attention appreciated all of the hard work and was supportive of my blog side project. Even though he didn't get what I was doing, he understood that it gave me inroads into the communities he wanted to tap. Sure, it was *just* social media, but it was the new way of the world. I knew it, he knew it, and we both knew that I knew more than him. Case in point: In 2017, markets who prioritized blogging efforts were thirteen times more likely to see positive ROI. We call that lucky number thirteen.

Bottom line, I was twenty-two, upgrading my life, on the right path, working hard, and paying dues.

And it was a big deal to me.

My parents are wholesale car dealers. We grew up middle class in Florida. They have never been to a fancy cocktail party or traveled outside of the United States. They referred to NYC as the "big city." They have owned and run their own business successfully for as long as I can remember (which is amazing to me; maintaining a marriage and a business for thirty years is no joke), and while they didn't go to college, they believe in the principle of hard and honest work and in-stilled that ethic within me and my sister, who also owns her own business.

So imagine my surprise when I discovered that hard and honest work wasn't always the ticket, or that nepotism and dollars can really get you any job, internship, or position you wanted. I was frustrated. My dad, unfortunately for me, didn't have an in-line to Anna Wintour. It took time for me to realize that even though you might be the best candidate, sometimes you're not the right political move within a company. Other people had one-ups and ins. I didn't know the busi-ness world wasn't based on a merit system. I didn't know about pedi-grees and rubbing elbows with the right people. I had the benefit of naïveté, which served me well multiple times in the beginning.

"You don't know what you don't know" can truly be a blessing.

Not a blessing? The *recession*.

I had left Attention after being poached by a larger company called IAC, a scary acronym for InterActiveCorp, to lead their "social media" efforts across multiple businesses but mainly their startup Pronto (a now-defunct Amazon competitor). That also came with a di-rector title, a six-figure salary, and a company that had an unlimited snack section and a built-in espresso bar.* I was moving up.

---

*We'll talk dollars, cents, and how to make sense of it all in the upcoming chapters, but I didn't want to drop the "six-figure salary" bomb like it's nothing (my parents were convinced I was doing something illegal when I told them what I was getting paid). I was an exception, making a

When Crushing it Crushes You

GRAM IT! TAG @WORKPARTY

And as it happens, amid my "crushing it," and nearly hitting corner-office goals, the recession hit, and the proverbial shit hit the fan for my career trajectory, and a lot of other people's. I was also in

---

salary not typically reserved for young people ripe with inexperience and questions about their 401(k) accounts. But sometimes, when you stumble upon a burgeoning marketplace (even in a recession) and have a unique, scalable skill set, you, too, will find yourself making serious dollars without serious experience.

the midst of ending a relationship, the end of my apartment lease happened to be coming up, and my company was downsizing quickly. All of these things made me feel like I was in the midst of a tornado with no way out.

One morning midtornado, I was called in for a meeting with the CEO of the company, and I thought, *This is it, I'm getting the ax.* So many questions ran through my head: Where would I go next? Was it a mistake to have left my last job? Did I still have the contact information of that high-up person at that other company who I might need to phone in a favor from?

But instead, the CEO presented me with two options: take a salary cut or be transferred to Los Angeles to a sister company, a company called Citysearch (think Yelp's older, unrulier brother), with the same job, same salary, same title.

At this point in my life, I had moved to three different cities solo—and I mean solo. So. Obviously. Lonely. Often. I didn't know one warm body in LA, which, however daunting, is an experience I highly recommend because part of being entrepreneurial is getting comfortable with being uncomfortable.

Well, I'd done it once, so I convinced myself I could do it again, rebuild from scratch. Start something new in a new city. I had never been to Los Angeles—in Florida, where I grew up, the West Coast wasn't the best coast. Admittedly, the knowledge I had was rife with stereotypes: entertainment flash, boobs, crystals, and a lot of health food. I was picturing movie LA, and I liked black turtlenecks, sarcasm, and the subway. And yet it sort of felt like the universe was pulling me in this direction. My gut was telling me it was time to do something potentially drastic, and my boss (who remains a friend and mentor to this day) really sold me on the whole SoCal package. And let's be real, I didn't have much of a choice. When people are getting fired left and right, and you get offered a new life without a pay down-grade? You take it.

Little did I know, that decision would set in motion a chain of events that have changed my life entirely. So I packed up my stuff, bid my besties farewell, and headed to La La Land. My safety net? Telling myself over and over again on the plane ride that I could always move back if this was one big epic fail.

Speaking of fail, I nearly missed my flight to California—an uncharacteristic near miss. Maybe fear of my impending LA life nearly got the best of me. Maybe I was procrastinating the logistics. I do know that I made my flight with minutes to spare and a ridiculously high resting heart rate. After what felt like the longest bicoastal flight imaginable, I landed in sunny SoCal eager to hit the ground running and make human friends.

I pulled up to my Koreatown loft, unpacked my clothing, and prepared for my first day at work. My new position was "basically" the same as my previous role, but my title was a little different, and that, well, that worried me from the very start. I went from being director of social media, a vertical I knew and understood in my core, to director of PR. Those two little letters have a lot of power, but at the time traditional PR efforts were a more antiquated approach to what I'd been doing. Our offices were on Sunset Boulevard in Hollywood, adding to the strange Los Angeles cliché I felt I was turning into.

But the whole executive team talked me off a ledge. I would be fine, they said. It's basically the same thing, they said.

pause

Let's call this out for what it is. Oftentimes in our careers when we feel like we have little choice in the matter, jobs or changes are positioned as "the same." They never are. No matter how similar something appears, you will never repeat the same role twice. When someone tells you same job, same responsibility, different title, take that with a healthy amount of skepticism and ask some tough questions. Like: Why is my title different? I wish I'd known to ask.

Uproot my whole life. Sure! Why not! What did I have to lose? Apparently a lot.

chapter two

Congrats on Your Failure

I went into my first day as director of PR at Citysearch confident and excited, bringing the same unfettered enthusiasm I had brought to my job in New York. I was excited to tackle working at a social network (a novel concept at the time), we had editors to vet user reviews and ratings, and the community would chime in as well. Three cheers for crowdsourced consumerism!

I knew what I was doing. I had done it all before (and in New York City, no less), but more and more, day in and day out, I felt like my voice was being shut down. My ideas were constantly being met with a head-cock and a "That's interesting, but . . ."

Basically, it was nothing like my previous role.

I remember being in a meeting pitching a few ideas, one of which was that we needed to put our editors out into the world more, make them social media celebrities or, as we know them now, influencers. This was the beginning of social, remember? Consumers wanted to know the people behind the brands and wanted to trust the experts (ahem, again, influencers). I was pushing social first, mobile check-ins (Foursquare had just launched), and really big-picture ideas, and I kept being told to "stick to my spreadsheet," filling in local news media email addresses. This was old-school PR.

Basically, I honed my Excel skills.

Idea after idea rejected, enthusiasm stuttered, but I kept pounding at the pavement, at the front door—I hollered through the window if it meant someone was listening. And look, of course I worried. You're only as valuable as the value you provide to the company, and in those moments, every time I hit a brick wall, I was at a value deficit. And yet I took the nos and kept moving forward, being slightly more aggressive in my approach.

Mistake. (Sort of.)

One morning an email from a higher-up female executive appeared in my in-box. "Suggestion" was the subject, as I recall. The body essentially said the following: "Your emails are coming off a little too aggressive." It continued, "I would add a smiley face when making requests of someone" ("someone" likely being my male counterpart). I think she was trying to be helpful in having me navigate the world as a female executive, but in turn, if you read between the lines, the suggestion was that I needed to be friendlier, more female, more passive. Honestly, the email shocked me. There I was, shimmying up the business-climbing rope, blisters and burns on my hands (because, let's be real, there's no ladder, that's far too easy), and I felt like I got the wind knocked out of me again, again, again, and again. I was doing my job and doing it well and getting shut down at every corner.

This "suggestion" was the email version of a guy on the sidewalk catcalling: "Why aren't you smiling?"

Were these emails being sent to my male counterparts? I doubt it. And yet I also knew that my direct tone in email correspondence was being misread as resting-bitch email. Men didn't end emails with x's and o's. They didn't send hearts or winking smiley faces. I thought we all ended our thoughts with good old-fashioned periods. A period was strong. Declarative. It commanded authority. I wanted authority, not qualifying statements or symbolic smiles.

Sorry, is there a difference?

"I need this by Wednesday." versus "Could I get this by Wednesday?"

There's a difference. A big difference. One asks for permission. And apparently permission is what I needed.

Now I don't know who the first perp was. Once reserved for Valentine's Day cards, *Gossip Girl*, and texts between friends, the "xoxo" trend was suddenly everywhere. Allegedly, even Diane Sawyer was using it. Multiple exclamation points adorned every exchange. At that point I didn't know it was possible to be THAT *excited!!!* about something.

I could have fought it, sure. I could have continued using periods on principle. TBH, I can't even recall how I responded, but the email has clearly stuck with me all these years. And that's when I realized, at every moment of your career, you can turn something frustrating into fuel. I thought, *If an exclamation point and a smiley face is what they need, sure. I will keep doing my job to the best of my ability and I'll customer-service the hell out of my correspondence.* So if you're going through hell, I say give 'em hell with an exclamation on top.

Now, with all that momentum and juice firing you up, you might be bummed to hear what happened next: I got laid off. Politely laid off. "Let's go for a walk" laid off. I wasn't a good "cultural fit." I was too eager. Too aggressive. They used all sorts of polite euphemisms, but alas, they said the position was no longer needed.

My first big blow, the whole life face-plant, was happening to me mid-upward-trajectory and "on my way." So I did what any twenty-three-year-old who has uprooted her entire life and moved cross-country, worked tirelessly and fiercely to establish her career, sacrificing her personal life in the mix to work harder than ever imaginable, would do: I fell apart.

Now, let's hit pause again because there's a bit of a plot twist. I would learn later there were many layers to me being let go from this position, one of which was a meeting with the CEO, my boss, and my then boyfriend . . . Let's just say, rock bottom is four levels lower than you ever thought. But for now, back to falling apart.

Look, truthfully, I love working hard. I had always identified as the girl who is crushing it career-wise, never the girl with the perfect hair and polished outfit, never the girl for whom it came easy—that's for damn sure. In fact, I remember a male colleague once telling me, "You're pretty, but not so pretty that other women will hate you." I made a confused face, and he followed up with, "No, no, that's a compliment and will get you far! You're not a threat!" Ugh, great! But now what? I—the striver, the try-hard, the career-woman—was in a city where I knew no one, had left behind connections, friends, and a promising career path to come kill it on the West Coast and then got laid off? Self. Identity. Screwed.

I was crushed. Devastated. And PRAISE BE social media hadn't hit its glorious stride yet, because this was not a 'Grammable moment or Facebook memory that you wanted to be reminded of. I did not need to livestream the depression that came next, nor did I need a feed of #goals to compare myself to.

Over the course of a career-based depressive episode, there are many moments when you will have to look at yourself in the mirror and opt for either a pep talk or pizza. I chose the latter, obviously. Extra cheese. All of the cheese. Every single time.

I slept in, stare-in-the-mirror-and-watch-yourself-cry cried, ordered pizza, stayed in pj's, repeat. I was ashamed, embarrassed, but also knew that I needed to pick myself up. (Note: This is not the first nor the last time this will happen. This cycle will lather, rinse, repeat for anyone who takes career and life risks, for that matter.)

About three weeks into Pizza Cry-Fest 2009, I begrudgingly emailed my contacts, letting them know I was free for work, looking for a job, and open for opportunities and was in . . . LA. Any career-driven woman knows what kind of sinking feeling I had hitting send on that email. I must have paced around for hours before that definitive and final click.

Once I sent that email, everyone would know I had failed. They'd *alllllllll* be talking about me. I'd be a joke: "Jackie moved to LA and thought she was gonna MAKE IT." At least that's what I thought. It's what we all tell ourselves when something goes wrong with our careers and life. But look, the reality is most of the time people *aren't* thinking about you. Sometimes they are. But the truth is, we women are so unbelievably hard on ourselves at moments of weakness, even though setbacks have happened to the best of us.

J. K. Rowling was rejected by publishers twelve times before someone said yes to *Harry Potter and the Sorcerer's Stone*. "Rock bottom," the best-selling author says, "became the solid foundation on which I rebuilt my life." At twenty-six, Anna Wintour was fired from *Harper's Bazaar*—"Everyone should be sacked at least once in their career," the *Vogue* editor-in-chief has said. Beyoncé lost a *Star Search* competition and eloquently put that audio into her best-selling album

because FUCK YES. Women never forget those kinds of moments. And while I'm neither the Ice Queen nor Queen Bey, I am an independent woman in a long line of women who have failed before they've succeeded. If you're in the setback portion of your story, I know that doesn't make it any easier. But there is solace in the shared experience with your role models.

People love to tell you their best biz advice is to "fail hard," but failure never feels good.

Instead of keeping my failure to myself, though, I knew I had to let the world know (or at least let MY world know) if I was ever going to move forward. This is where that "sit down, write the email, be humble" voice should pop into your head. You can peak several times in your career—I thought I was on track to be a vice president by the time I was thirty, and I got let go—but success is not linear anymore, and neither is the industry or the work we're doing.

So I did what I didn't want to do: I admitted failure. And guess what? The world didn't end. My career wasn't over. To the contrary, it was only beginning.

Leap, Then Look

One of the first things I did after I lost my job was read and find solace in *The 4-Hour Workweek*. In it, *New York Times* best-selling author Tim Ferriss talks about how sometimes being capable can be a curse. When I look back at all of the traits that make me a great CEO now—thinking ahead, getting work done efficiently and moving on to the next thing, making decisions and delegating, being ambitious and able to pivot on a dime—they weren't always the best fit for super corporate environments. If you recognize these traits in yourself, you might be bound for entrepreneurial greatness—90 percent of millennials surveyed think being an entrepreneur means having a certain mind-set rather than starting a company. Also, know that at least once in your career, the thing that makes you great will be the thing that gets you fired.

Plenty of companies are stuck in the mud, doing things the old way. And I get it, women and men at the top don't want twenty-somethings rolling into the workplace talking about something they don't know about, and it's easy to get shut down.

I knew I didn't want to do anything the old way. I wanted to take my talents and strengths to create new business opportunities for myself and my clients. Shortly after I sent out that "taking on work" email, responses started to roll back in slowly but surely.

The good news? I wasn't totally screwed. I had severance and ten times cheaper rent than in New York. I also had kept Some Notes on Napkins alive during my move, and brands were starting to look at blogging as more than just a hobby. For two months, I kept on blogging, taking random deals like an on-air gig as a style host on a commercial interstitial with TBS (during which I frankly had no idea what I was doing—thankfully this is not on the internet). I was also starting to get sent products to write about—again, not cash, but it was something.

I was working from home and freelancing various marketing gigs for several months. I had no pals. I had pizza. I would literally go to the gym just to find some human interaction and, duh, work off the pizza (#single). One night, to beat the boredom and try and make new friends, I took myself out for a blogger meetup event hosted in the Fashion District and I met someone.

No, not that kind of someone. Even better. She was a soon-to-be fellow entrepreneur, Amanda, who was on the verge of quitting her day job, looking to launch her business in events and go freelance as well.

We were both young, social go-getters. The normal "What do you do?" question came up, and before I knew it, Amanda told me she was looking into getting an office space to launch her event business and asked if I wanted in. Since at this point the elliptical was my BFF, meeting Amanda felt like another push in the right direction from the universe. Also, for anyone who is from NYC, the thought of office space feels totally out of reach, but all the sudden it wasn't. Plus, someone once said there is nothing more expensive than a missed opportunity, so I wasn't about to say no.

So I leapt without looking. Or, perhaps a little less cliché, has anyone ever heard of spatial disorientation? There's this thing where pilots aren't supposed to look down at the ground while they're flying because they will instinctively tip the nose of the plane down. Just keep flying, just keeping flying. And that's what I was doing. No looking down.

Before I knew it, Amanda and I had office space. It was 2010, and we were working out of our very own space in Downtown Los Angeles—it wasn't as glamorous as it sounds, that's for sure. The guy on the top floor was hosting raves on the weekend. The second floor was some bizarro-land artists' commune/gallery space with a woodworking area. One morning, while I walked into the building, a man

looked me right in the eyes as he performed his "morning ablutions"—
to put it politely.

We shared the space with a dude who had invested all of his bar
mitzvah money in Apple stock and was now making alternative music
videos and documentaries on Joshua Tree. But it didn't matter, we had
two thousand square feet of loft space that cost $800 a month. There
was no AC, but we were living our dream, sweating it out together in
plastic Ikea chairs.

We were excited, being scrappy, taking a risk and reaping small
rewards. We got an intern. We were learning about each other's
business—mine, at the time, being primarily marketing and social
media and hers being event production. We were gleefully yippee-
ing together after any email back we got. We started thinking of
names to call our space, creatives to bring into the mix. It was us,
cheap furniture, laptops, and unfettered enthusiasm propelling us
forward into an unknown and exciting space (metaphorically and literally).

In the beginning we weren't business partners—we simply shared
a space. But that soon changed when we began approaching prospective clients together, under one name.

For the sake of storytelling, let's refer to the small marketing shop
we set up as Serious Business Venture 1.0. I really wish I had taken it
in more at the time, because you'll never feel more unsure, naïve, or
excited by what could happen than when you first start out on your
own with a brand-new company of your own devising. We barely had
any clients, just a few local bars and businesses that came to us to
help them grow their online communities, which we were eager to do.
Happy hour would start at 4 p.m., when we'd walk to Cole's in Downtown Los Angeles and have Pimm's cups.

pause

For those of you who are in this moment: Cherish it, celebrate it, it will probably never get better or purer than that moment. You only get to have a first kiss once. Same goes for your first company. There is only one beginning.

As time in the space went on, we realized that two service lines are better than one, and that we'd be stronger together. So we joined forces and started an official company. I knew NOTHING. Or as close to nothing as humanly possible. I can still hear the LegalZoom partnership agreement printing from our slow AF printer. We both signed the agreement fast, furiously, and went out to our daily happy hour to celebrate. Agreement signed, Pimm's cups up!

We were now CEOs.

chapter three

What Have You Got to Lose?

(Apparently a Lot)

We got right down to business.

First, Amanda and I made a list of dream companies we wanted to work with: Taschen, Levi's, and Baxter of California landed at the top. And a ton of opportunities started to roll in, partly based on the reputation that I had made for myself. (See: later this chapter how you are your reputation—and don't forget it. That needs to be a sticking point for every single entrepreneur.)

During the first months of our newfound partnership, I found myself speaking on a panel at a preeminent fashion trade show on social media and the digital landscape. About 1,500 brands took over a massive convention center in Las Vegas. A fashion trade show is where everyone from buyers and bloggers to press and designers congregate to select the next season's trends. Brands wanted tastemakers. Social was top of mind.

I had clarity and vision into this world and knew that it all comes back to dollars and reputation. At that panel, I dropped what's since become a Jackie-ism—something I had no idea would garner such a reaction. I simply said, "Rule number one: Be a fucking pleasure to work with." It's true! There will be people better than you or cheaper than you. But if people like working with you, they will always come back. I've drilled it into my employees, colleagues, and counterparts for good reason.

Post panel, the president of the trade show approached me and said bluntly, "I want to hire you as our director of marketing." A momentary flash went through my head: Steady paycheck, bicoastal lifestyle—this could be a really solid adult move. What everyone knows today as #adulting.

So when I found myself saying the complete opposite, instead forming the sentence "Don't hire me, hire my agency," it was as much of a shock to me as it was to him.

Before I knew it, Amanda and I were on a plane to New York City for our first big pitch, all for our newly formed and somewhat nonexistent agency. It was the perfect opportunity for us to do it together and figure it out as we went along.

Which reminds me of one of my favorite pieces of advice, from none other than digital media mogul Hillary Kerr, cofounder of Clique Media Group. Hillary didn't start out as a media mogul. She started as an editor at *Elle*, a job she left to launch a little site you might know as Who What Wear, followed by Byrdie, MyDomaine, and more with fellow editor and cofounder Katherine Power.

Leaving cushy and respectable editorial jobs at a top fashion magazine to become entrepreneurs might sound completely exhilarating, exciting, and par for the fashion course to people now, but Katherine and Hillary launched back in 2006. Amazon was still known mostly as a bookseller then, LOL. MySpace was king, and most leading fashion magazines had only splash pages as websites, with no content at all.

And yet that's what the fashion power duo did. After meeting on the set of the show *Project Runway* while working for *Elle*, they struck up a friendship and bonded immediately; within a year they had started the Who What Wear newsletter as the answer to the lack at the time of great editorial content online. That's right, Hillary and Katherine saw an opportunity (whitespace!) and took a leap (before they looked!): They left their jobs at *Elle* and launched a newsletter, which has now become the Clique Media Group media empire.

Speaking to our audience at Create & Cultivate Dallas, Hillary said, "Say yes and figure it out." That was her strategy in the beginning: *Say yes and figure it out.* Simple, yet powerful.

For budding female entrepreneurs, it's perfect advice for two reasons: (1) Why not? And (2) you're never going to have all your ducks in a row or the experience you "need." So all you need, at least at the onset, is the gusto to say yes. *Confidence begets confidence.*

Which is exactly what we did after I made my bold statement. We said yes. I said, "Hire my nonexistent company." And instead of saying no, the president said, "Fly to New York and pitch me." WHAT? It was crazy. We didn't have a site or business cards. I simply had a notion in my head that we could do it. Was I terrified? Abso-fucking-lutely. Let me repeat. Absolutely. Who wouldn't be? But . . .

We figured it out.

This would be our first big fish. All we had to do is reel him in. But where do you start? How do you know what to ask for? These are all questions you go over again and again, and there is no playbook, certainly not for young, green female entrepreneurs. But you cannot build confidence without stepping off the cliff.

TBH, I stepped off that cliff very blind.

In fact, I went off backward.

This isn't the part of the story where I tell you I mirror-practiced my pitch. I never recited affirmations. I didn't have note cards that I shuffled through nervously on the plane ride to New York. Pitching is a weird art form and definitely falls into the "you get better over time" category. It's a craft I like to think I have honed into a skill. So how did I prepare?

Here are my tricks and tips on how to be pitch-perfect:

1. Memorize your elevator pitch and be able to deliver it with ease. Just one or two sentences that describe precisely what your company does and what your value proposition is.

2. Know who is going to be in the room and know more about them than they know about you. Then use that information to create common ground and a shared language. For example: "I saw you attended NYU, I know you worked on that project," etc.

3. Know your competitors as well as your own business and be able to speak to both eloquently.

4. Know what differentiates you from your competitors and talk about that, too.

5. Understand the business of the person you are pitching and be able to throw around stats and recent campaigns you thought performed well and be able to say why.

6. Read the room, and know when to move on from a slide and/or an idea if they aren't loving it.

7. If you're sitting down, find a reason to stand up. Changing their line of sight will refresh the room's vibe and create a little momentum.

A SUCCINCT AND PERSUASIVE STATEMENT ON YOUR COMPANY

8. Arm yourself with your biggest wins and key references that will give you a glowing referral (case studies are key!).

9. Be prepared to talk money and, more importantly, why

you charge what you charge; people want to understand the number, and if they can understand it, they will pay it.

10. Get your story straight. If you are going to be in the room with other people from your team, make sure you are on the same page with any details. (In our case, how many employees do you have? Amanda said three. I said four. Lesson learned.)

You might be thinking, *But I'm not good at any of what you just listed. I get nervous and I forget information.* No one starts out pitch-perfect. Not even Anna Kendrick. You will make mistakes nearly every time you get up to pitch. You'll forget a stat that you've repeated ten thousand times. You'll read the room entirely wrong. You will bore people to tears. And when they start looking at their phones, my god, it's a gut punch you have to take without anyone noticing.

Which is where imposter syndrome sneaks into your brain. It creeps in the shadows at first. Lingers in the corners of your mind. The scary ghost under the bed. Comes out at the most inopportune times—like on a flight to New York (that city you left with big career aspirations, only to get fired) when you start to wonder, *Why would they hire us? Is a $10K retainer too much to ask for? They could hire a major firm, so why choose us?* And then the kid in the seat behind you gives you a much-needed kick to snap you out of it. *Of course you can do this. You KNOW this. You GOT THIS.*

And look, imposter syndrome is real. Fear of personal failure was the number one fear in a 2016 poll of Americans—and for millennials and women, this fear is often masked as imposter syndrome, which can be defined as the feeling of being inadequate despite continued success. A whopping 70 percent of millennials experience this, in both work and life, but why?

It might be because, as one expert put it, we entered the work-force at a time of "outrageous technological advancements and constant comparison on social media," um, yup.

This shouldn't come as a major shock. The onslaught of tech has made many millennials in the workforce feel like they can't ever get a grasp on their job or their #grammable life as they open their mail to find more and more student-loan bills. Just when you feel like you've figured it all out, something new comes along and wipes your career slate clean. Which is exactly what entrepreneurship feels like most days.

In part, one of the reasons I felt so much pressure on that plane was because I was returning to the city I had left. It felt like I had to prove myself to myself. One firing wasn't going to define me. To the contrary, I'd be like a freaking phoenix rising from the ashes—or, rather, a woman on a plane rising from the LA smog. Either/or.

They don't prepare you for imposter syndrome in business school. No one tells you about the pep talks you'll need to give yourself or the realities of founder depression. Another Create & Cultivate favorite, Jeni Britton Bauer, founder and CEO of Jeni's Splendid Ice Creams, once said, "The last thing you want to do as an entrepreneur is go to business school." You can teach business, but you can't teach vision. And though Jeni knows a thing or two about packing a pint, hitting the sweet spot didn't come easy. There were learning curves, major lessons, and hard, trailblazing work. "Every entrepreneur has a very different experience, but one thing is always true: You get a wacky idea that becomes a vision and then you start working toward that vision and never quit. No matter what," she says. "Entrepreneurship can be extraordinarily isolating; the better your idea is, the more people will be repelled by it. When

I started, no one wanted spicy ice cream, or flower petal or herb ice cream. It's about getting help from anyone you can and proving yourself over time. You are the only one who will champion your idea, and in some ways, that never ends."

Jeni is a solid example of a woman who has found success precisely because she didn't play by the rules. She's been in business for over two decades and has over twenty stores now. And yet she still believes, "We will get better as we grow, not the other way around."

I don't have an MBA. I didn't go to business school. But I do have an unnerving amount of drive that allows me to take chances on ideas I have. Create & Cultivate started as twenty-five people at the Ace Hotel in Palm Springs. It's now thousands of women in a room and a community of five hundred thousand women interacting daily. You have to be able to visualize the dream. And I saw it for me. Even if I wasn't entirely sure of what "the dream" was, I knew it could be huge.

In every career there are trends, but rules that apply to traditional careers don't apply when you've launched your own business. You have to think about the current marketplace and the platform that you're using. *Pretty Woman* was an amazing rom-com in 1990. Make that movie today and you'd get skewered. Big mistake. HUGE.

We knew that we had to leap. For us, that pitch in New York was our shining moment, because we landed our first fish. And then we really started cooking. Post pitch, we sat in that moment of silence: Did we win? Did we lose? Should we leave? And then we heard four simple words: "Where do we sign?" From there we were off! We were producing events and social media campaigns for the likes of Levi's and Marimekko and throwing incredible events with people like Mark Ronson and Rosario Dawson. We were workpartying our way to the top.

———————

There were cringe-worthy moments, of course. Once we got our first business credit card, we took out one of our favorite (and highest-paying) clients to Soho House West Hollywood. At the time, Soho House West Hollywood was the be-all-end-all place you wanted to wine and dine new clients. So I applied and spent way too much money on a membership that I couldn't afford/couldn't believe had been accepted. I felt slightly out of place every time I stepped into Soho's amazing space. The leather booths. The wraparound terrace. The IG-worthy dining room where no photos are allowed. You're having dinner thirty stories up, overlooking the city of dreams. You're literally all the way up. And I had to remind myself I belonged there. (Hello, imposter syndrome. It was always there to knock me out of the tower.) And our card was DECLINED. People's cards don't get declined at exclusive membership clubs like Soho House. The waiter was totally polite, but definitely wasn't used to dealing with declines.

There was no reason for it, just a glitch in the system, but OMG, I was mortified and horrified. Should I have been so upset? Was it really a game-changer? No. If someone didn't want to hire me because of a glitch in a system, then it probably wouldn't turn into a great long-term working relationship.

But at the same time, when you're just starting, you feel like you're under a microscope. That you will be found out at any minute. Any second. Little situations like that will pop up daily and teach you (slowly) how to stay calm under pressure and laugh it off. Your face may be on fire, but your body language has to keep saying, "My biz is on fire."

From not pulling the right fire permits in time to launch a very fancy store in Beverly Hills (but somehow convincing the fire marshal to let us throw it anyway), to not having the budget for cleaning staff post event and scrubbing every last dish by hand, we made the most of every moment. The time leading up to the event is always work—eyes-burning, heart-racing, palms-sweating work—but in the moment when you realize you've pulled it off, when you glance around a room and see people having a blast, there's euphoria knowing you've done it. Whatever felt impossible before, you've conquered. It's well-earned exhaustion. It fills you with pride and happiness. It's like getting an A at life. That's a WorkParty.

At moments, Amanda and I were CEOs, and at others we were bartenders, waitstaff, cleaning crew, and security; you do anything and everything to keep your events on budget, the lights on, and the client happy. Or we certainly did. Being "yes-women" might sound contrary to some of my advice—know when to push back, know when to say no—advice that every working woman has heard at this point. But when you're growing, the time to say no is before the signed contract and cashed check. Once you've accepted the terms, you need to get ready to say yes—and say yes with a smile no matter what is asked of you (with an exclamation point)!

Despite roadblocks and hiccups here and there, two years into Serious Business Venture 1.0, we were growing, we were thriving, and we were working with dream clients. (Again, #workparty.) We were taking conference calls with clients that I had put on my dream list. I was learning all about the event industry and creatively thinking about how to integrate offline and online experiences, as people began to expect in the new era of social media. And I was having the time of my life.

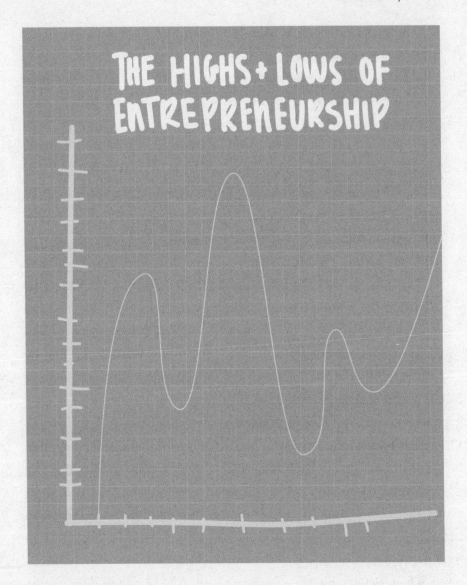

Let's break for an inspirational quote: "Don't call them dreams. Call them plans."

I had plans.

Amanda and I had scraped by together. We were doing it. Spit, glue, and whatever else it took. This is why it's called sweat equity. If there's no sweat in your hustle, you're not hustling hard enough. We were growing and hiring.

And . . . YES, imposter syndrome and snafus aside . . . I finally referred to myself as an entrepreneur.

And it felt unreal.

––––––––––––

"I am an entrepreneur." Those are four very important words to speak out loud. Remember, confidence begets confidence. You should bookend your crazy thoughts with those four words.

I AM AN ENTREPRENEUR.

Pep talk to self: *This is what an entrepreneur looks like.* That woman in the mirror. The one saying yes and figuring it out. The one confidently putting one unconfident foot in front of the other. *Oh my gosh, what am I doing? What did I get myself into? What if they find me out? Or will I fail?* No. You won't fail. Or you might. Either way, you're going after it. You're doing it.

I AM AN ENTREPRENEUR.

Entrepreneur is a title you bestow on yourself and something that I didn't take lightly—I felt like I had earned my imaginary badge. No one ever says to you, "Hey! You're an entrepreneur, did you know that?" It's something you have to muster up some gumption to say to yourself, first in the mirror and then to others. "Hey, Jackie, you're an entrepreneur." Say it to yourself a million times.

The official name of someone who refers to herself in third person is an illeist. Most famous illeists are men. The Rock. Bob Dole. Elmo. Which is definitely cute. But if you think about it, little kids do it all the time: "Andy wants a cookie." "Maya wants to watch TV." And little kids, as some of you know, are the best negotiators. They win all the time.

During difficult situations, like the first two years of launching a biz, talking to yourself in third person can actually help calm you down. According to a study published in the journal *Scientific Reports*, talking about yourself to yourself is a way to make that internal monologue useful.

The study explains, "Although people frequently engage in such 'self-talk,' recent findings indicate that the language they use to refer to the self when they engage in this process influences self-control. Specifically, using one's own name to refer to the self during introspection, rather than the first-person pronoun 'I,' increases people's ability to control their thoughts, feelings, and behavior under stress."

Those pep talks you give yourself in the morning? Do it in third person, with either your own name or a pronoun like "you," "he," or "she." Or do it before you're about to step into a big presentation to calm your jitters. Practice and see what happens to your nerves when you make the switch.

Go from something like this:

"I can do this. I know this material and I'm ready to go in and show them."

To something like this:

"You can do this. You know this material and you're ready to go in and show them."

In the second-person example, you become your own best friend. And if you're your own best friend, you can never be betrayed (a lesson I was about to learn).

I thought I had launched a biz with a BFF—someone whom I could trust with my professional reputation, someone who had my back no matter what, someone who was going to be around for a long time. But what goes up must come down.

When I look back now, I can see that there were some warning signs of what was to come, none of which I saw at the time. At this point, Amanda and I had had two good years together. But we'd had a conversation early on, one where we talked about what we each wanted out of the business long-term. My answer then remains true today: I wanted to grow a business, work for myself, and have the creative autonomy of being my own boss. Oh, and get more cool clients, of course.

Amanda's answer was blunt: money. She wanted to make a lot of money. Let me be clear: There's nothing wrong with wanting to make a lot of money. Women are so often chastised for admitting that they are running a for-profit business. But unless you are running a nonprofit, your biz should make money (and even in a nonprofit, you should be in the black!). Looking back, her dollar dreams weren't the problem. The problem is that we didn't talk about how much money, where that money was coming from, and how we were spending that money. We weren't on the same page.

Money is an uncomfortable topic for most people. And as a twenty-something businesswoman, I wasn't equipped to have that conversation and just assumed that we were both on the same page when it came to the dollars and cents of the business.

But the way she wanted money was different from the way I wanted it. That's probably where our biggest discrepancy was. By nature, I am a financially risk-averse entrepreneur. I was developing money habits then that have carried into my business today. For instance, I don't like owing people money. I don't count my money chickens before they hatch, and I like the comfort of knowing I can pay employee salaries on time. At that point, Serious Business Venture 1.0 had two or three employees, and we were paying ourselves the lowest possible salary to reinvest what we were making back into the company. I'm pretty sure none of us had health insurance. I approached cash flow conservatively, with an air of caution and my accountant mother's voice constantly in my head saying, "Did you save the receipt?!" Our expenses were low. I charged my daily parking to the company, and that's pretty much it.

Amanda was expensing, well, a whole lot of things. And I had no idea. How is that possible, you ask? She would send me monthly projections, and they looked good to me because the projections were good, but what was actually happening on the back end was a different story. And my mistake was that I didn't ask to dig deeper. I didn't question her—I wasn't the finance person; she was. That was part of our deal (and my bad for not having those tough money conversations up front). I wasn't involved in the day-to-day finances at all. We'd always agreed that she would do finances and I'd handle creative—and honestly, I never thought we'd be making the kind of money we were that quickly. Having access to that much capital was a slippery slope for her, and I don't think she realized it until after the fact.

I didn't realize it either until one day over two years in.

Every morning I drove to our office in my Prius and paid five dollars to park in the lot. "Good morning, good morning, how are you this morning?" the attendant asked every morning, like we were meeting for the first time, every single day. You had to have five dollars cash or you couldn't park. The lot policy was no ins and outs, and he wouldn't give us any breaks. I remember so much about that office, those years, that intense propulsion of success laced with underlying fear and lack of experience in the mix. And I definitely remember that parking attendant.

That morning I drove to the office. "Good morning, good morning," the attendant said as I handed over a wrinkled five-dollar bill.

I'd recently begun experiencing a sinking feeling, the one you get in the pit of your stomach when you suspect your business partner is taking meetings with your contacts without you, the one where screens shrink the moment you walk in the door, the one where you feel that something is absolutely wrong and it can't be ignored any longer. And at around that same time, a friend suggested that maybe I should get more involved in the finances, so that morning I dusted off the old password spreadsheet and logged into our Citibank account. Right away, a couple of initial charges struck me as odd. Dinner at a trendy Los Angeles restaurant from the week prior for more than one hundred dollars. I remembered her telling me she had dinner with our friend John that night, someone whom I loved dearly but who wasn't involved in our business in any way whatsoever. *Maybe they talked business?* I thought. But then I kept scrolling.

Online shopping purchases.

Flights and hotel rooms for non-business-related travel.

Random cash withdrawals.

I started to freak out and printed out every month's statement, grabbing a highlighter and frantically highlighting every charge that was a mystery to me.

Unexplainable expensive trips to Target.

Here I was diligently expensing my "five dollars, no ins, no outs" parking.

There had to be a reasonable explanation.

A friend arrived home that night to find papers scattered around me, highlighter in hand. I must have looked like a maniac surrounded by these bright yellow papers.

I had gone deep. And I had found the one. The expense that pushed me over the edge.

She had bought my birthday present with the company's money.

Maybe she justified it by reasoning that some expenses were meant for keeping up appearances. At the time, I was still making money from Some Notes on Napkins and being sent swag. Maybe she thought she deserved more of a cut? That this was somehow normal, or would make some sort of sense? I had never expensed one dinner without her explicit consent in a prior conversation, and in total that may have been once or twice (except for the parking).

I was *devastated*. Remember when I said rock bottom keeps going? I was deep in the earth's core and had no clue how to "break up" with a friend—much less a business partner.

Shortly after I got up off the highlighter-strewn floor, I did what all women do when they need advice. I called my mom. Then I hired a lawyer and a forensic accountant (no, I had never heard of them before either; my lawyer told me I needed one). The partnership was over. Clearly. We were gonna break up. (Cue: not a #workparty.) Slowly but surely, Bill, my forensic accountant, uncovered more and more items, enough to build a case for Amanda and me to part ways.

After months of internally groveling and trying to come to grips both personally and professionally with what was happening, we finally had our tough convo. It ended in her leaving the company. There was, of course, back and forth. And the ending negotiations were made even more difficult by our lack of an agreement setting forth our operating responsibilities in writing.

But contrary to the popular saying, I believe that you *are* your failures. Not in a dramatic way. Not in a soul-crushing way. Your failures can define you in a rad way if you are brave enough to let them. And if hindsight is 20/20, you might as well look back on those failures with some chic glasses.

Every single failure and fuckup becomes part of your story and trajectory. The lesson is always there. I would have never become an entrepreneur if I had never met Amanda or if I'd never been let go. Honestly, Serious Business Venture 1.0 felt safer because I had a partner. In retrospect, meeting her was the best and worst thing that ever happened to me.

The amazing thing is, after something like that happens, you—

and you alone—own the narrative. Nothing has to level you, but the lesson is that you do have to have those tough conversations.

Ending the friendship, however, didn't come with legal paperwork. That was painful. It was tear-soaked. There was nothing to sign, no dotted line or tidy way to end a friendship. To build a business with someone from scratch, only to have it break into a million pieces broke me. I won't deny that I blared that annoying song "Now you're just somebody that I used to know . . ." and casually, sporadically ugly-cried in my Prius.

So I'm passing on my six major takeaways from this oh-so-teachable moment:

1. Your Reputation Is Your Résumé.

Spend the early part of your career building relationships. They don't need to be with top dogs or CEOs, but rather, start with the people around you. Be good to them. Work hard with them. Become the worker that they suggest to clients when they move on to a new job. Without your reputation, you have a piece of paper. And what good is that?

2. Work Your Network.

There's a reason it's called net-*work*. Life is a group project. If you don't know where to start, send out an email. It killed me to send the email saying that I was open to freelance work and taking on clients. But sit down, write the email, be humble, and reach out to the people you know who can help. It will come full circle.

3. Get It in Writing.

When someone doesn't put their word in writing, there's a reason. You can't produce a handshake in court. You can't file a motion against a hug. Get everything in writing and notarized. No matter how small or seemingly trivial the deal point is, without a paper trail, you're not getting that paper.

4. Read the Whole Contract (and Understand It).

Do you know what an operating agreement is? We had a 50/50 LLC, but we didn't have an agreement clearly setting out respective responsibilities. You should have an operating agreement that may change over time and that clearly outlines the roles you and your partners play in the business. Our agreement didn't say anything about her being in charge of the finances. If you don't want to pay attention and learn the words you don't understand, you're going to go down at one point or another.

5. Take Your Creative Project Seriously.

Without Some Notes on Napkins, I would have found myself in a much more precarious financial situation. Luckily, I had taken my blog seriously from day one. I created my own spreadsheet and had multiple revenue streams that helped me and continue to help me. If you're spending time on it, it's worth treating like a real business.

6. Learn about Your Relationship to Money and Have the Hard Convos Early.

Amanda and I should have had conversations (that we then put in writing) about what is considered a business expense and what is considered a personal expense, but I avoided that for two whole years. And as someone wisely put it, I learned what could have been a million dollar lesson for far less. Painful, nonetheless.

The last few years had been a rocky road. I had put myself out there. I had visualized what my dream career would look like, and I had presumably launched it with Amanda. I grew my professional reputation and signed dream clients. I was on top of my game. And then I was at the bottom. But you know what they also say that's so true it's nearly inevitable?

Once you hit below rock bottom, there's nowhere to go but up.

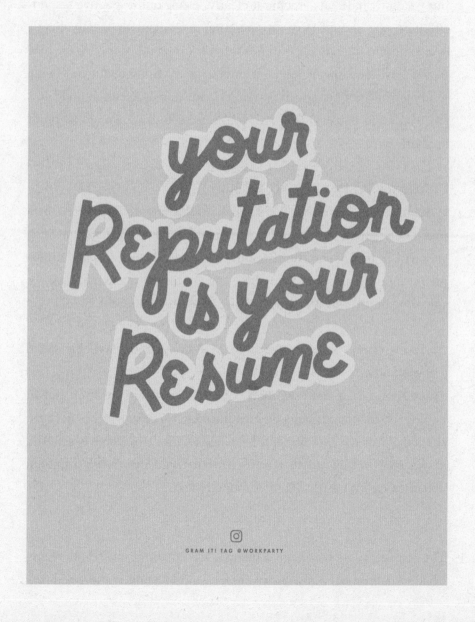

your Reputation is your Resume

GRAM IT! TAG @WORKPARTY

chapter four

The Comeback Kid-ult

Enter the Comeback Year. Yes, I can confirm the alleged pendulum DOES swing the other way. And when a girl comes back from the bicoastal move, broken relationship, layoff, business launch, and business-partner separation, she has to be strategic with her energy, not unlike Stella on her quest to get her groove back.

And for me personally, this included moving out of Los Angeles for a few months, buying what is, IMO, a therapy dog named Noah Wiley, and strategically freaking out over what my next step was with the business.

The silver lining of being a solo CEO is that you get to rebuild your brand on your own terms. This should be a fun, experimental, and aspirational exercise. You get to picture what you want your business to look like, how you want it to be perceived, and what will set you apart. Do not underestimate the importance of this work! These ideas are the blueprints you'll come back to when you're doubting yourself or the business. This exercise is an emotional labor, and as shallow as it may sound, you need to be invested in the perception of your business.

Serious Business Venture 1.0 and my partnership with Amanda accelerated in 2013. It was an early 2000s marketing era, one where the Bebas font family reigned supreme and millennial pink was on the upswing.

The business, now run by an in-over-my-head-but-keeping-it-mostly-together me, was legitimate and growing with a little elbow grease and hustle. After the business divorce and the chunk of time where I had to tell people about said divorce (read: clients, contacts, mutual friends), the dust started to settle. I maintained the majority of our retainer clients, and life, along with the business, moved on.

Our breakup had happened mostly behind closed doors, and our small team had been spared most of my headaches and heartache. It was isolating as hell, but I felt like I'd just gained a valuable lesson in boundaries and, more importantly, when to establish them. I wanted my team of three to see me as a leader, not a flailing twenty-something or the "hot mess" female protagonist that was permeating culture and entertainment at the time.

I'd often lead a status meeting or client call and then need to take ten in our office's industrial, high-ceilinged bathroom that looked out onto South Los Angeles Avenue and cry my eyes out. I am not the first woman—nor will I be the last—to seek solace in the women's restroom at work. The women's room acts as a patriarchal shield, a safe space for tears, and a place to be vulnerable. It was the only place I felt I could be vulnerable from nine to six. It just felt like so much, too much, to handle alone.

I realized that my business's reputation was only as strong as I built it up to be, and this was the time to puff my feathers and learn the not-so-subtle art of peacocking. We were a hard-to-define business, a square peg in the marketing agency round hole, but the responsibility and the vision were mine.

I set out to yet again find this elusive whitespace that I've now mentioned in this book.

Let's start with my definition of whitespace so that we're all on the same page, literally and figuratively. I define whitespace as the unique value your business adds to an industry. I'm sure there are hundreds of economics textbooks that have formal names for this, like "value proposition" or "value add." And, yes, that's at the core of whitespace. But so is innovation, another concept probably referred to as "disruption" in those same textbooks. I think of whitespace as a canvas of opportunity, as more of an emotional and instinctual theory than a line item in a dense business plan. Ideas have the power to disrupt the status quo if they are powerful enough and touch on a human insight. Just look at how the rise of the sharing economy has upended the taxi and hotel industries in the last five years. Think about crowdsourced funding and how that has fundamentally changed the arts and their respective fandoms. The list goes on and on.

So how can you find whitespace? You have to ask yourself the following burning questions:

✦ What can I do differently from others?

✦ What does currently not exist that would serve a specific need?

✦ What is an open arena to make money? How are people *not* capitalizing on something?

✦ What are some characteristics that are unique to me, and how can I manifest those in my business?

✦ What is my point of view on said specific industry, and how is it different from others?

✦ How can I achieve my goals authentically, creatively, efficiently, and effectively while maintaining what makes me unique?

I had to reinvent the company and myself at this juncture, and in the process, I had to "iterate my business model" (a phrase that, as an

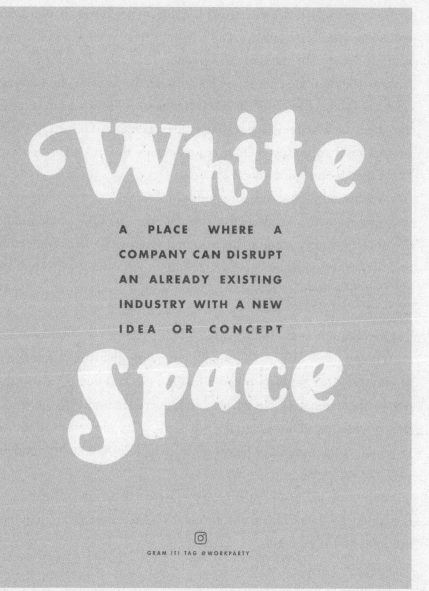

White

A PLACE WHERE A
COMPANY CAN DISRUPT
AN ALREADY EXISTING
INDUSTRY WITH A NEW
IDEA OR CONCEPT

Space

GRAM IT! TAG @WORKPARTY

entrepreneur, you will develop a love/hate relationship with; it basically just means "pivot"). I want to note here that this is a fucking
hard process, and it's absolutely harder as a woman.

Breaking into a male-dominated industry (is that not every industry?) is not impossible, but it will require longer hours, harder work, and some kind of sedative for all the imposter syndrome talks you're going to have with yourself. In October 2017, the *Harvard Business Review* released the first study to definitively disprove that women "lack confidence" or don't "lean in" or whatever other reason is trending about lack of female workplace advancement. The study placed sensors on men and women at one company to track their behavior. What they found won't shock you.

"We found almost no perceptible differences in the behavior of men and women," the study explains. "Women had the same number of contacts as men, they spent as much time with senior leadership, and they allocated their time similarly to men in the same role." And yet—oh boy, here it comes—"women weren't advancing and men were."

Say that out loud: *And yet women weren't advancing and men were.*

The study went on: "Our analysis suggests that the difference in promotion rates between men and women in this company was due not to their behavior but to how they were treated. This indicates that arguments about changing women's behavior—to 'lean-in,' for example—might miss the bigger picture: Gender inequality is due to bias, not differences in behavior."

Bias. Not differences in behavior. It's both a breath of fresh air to read and, still, incredibly painful. And it's something that women have put up with f-o-r-e-v-e-r.

Forever.

When you walk into a room and can count the number of women on one hand, that hand might tremble. But as long as you stick it out and assert your authority in that room, the number of women-owned businesses will continue to rise. And rising they are, even in the face of bias.

Between 1997 and 2006, businesses fully- or majority-owned by women grew at nearly twice the rate of all US firms (42.3 percent versus 23.3 percent).

That growth is the opposite of NBD. That growth is HEY, PRETTY BIG DEAL. #PBD. We're doing it and we're doing it with 2 percent of total venture capital funding. (Yes, you read that right: The amount of venture money that goes to female companies is only 2 percent.) But ladies, it's getting better. Not easier, but better.

It gets better . . . *with time*. You get better with time. Doubting yourself, your abilities, your worth—it's normal when you're trying to make a business. But you get better at calming your own nerves and presenting yourself—and your ideas—with confidence (the true c-word).

So I set out to rebuild and lean into these new areas of marketing and experiences. I had scattered intellectual property, a business that now had three full-time employees and a rotation of freelancers and an accountant (a.k.a. my mother) whom I could trust. And that was my stake in Los Angeles. A business that was starting to look less and less like smoke and mirrors and more and more like dollars and sense, a new big-girl apartment, an adorable therapy dog, a new anti-anxiety prescription, and an increasingly strained relationship with my accountant.

Ads Before #Ads

As far as the business of Serious Business Venture 1.0 was concerned, I refocused on disruptive service offerings, finding that bloggers (now dubbed influencers) were growing more into the marketing mainstream. Brands were starting to realize the power of content and the creators behind it. Until this point, bloggers were seen as people to invite to your brand's pop-up or party, not a group of media powerhouses with loyal fanbases that could not only drive sales but also crash sites.

I revisited my company's elevator pitch, completely revising the purpose of our business and the two-year-old mission statement. This is the sort of iterating you have to get comfortable with. This is the tough-love portion of the program where I tell you, in no uncertain terms: If you're not pivoting, you're not paying attention.

I think it's also important to give some context for this moment in time. It was the Wild West of blogging, and the term "influencer" was a buzzword people still got excited about. This was pre-#ad and pre-#spon. It felt like a graduating class of bloggers, all women in their twenties of different shapes, sizes, backgrounds, and races, putting what they liked out in the world. Now it feels passé, but sharing what made me tick for almost seven years was a beautiful thing. I had people who knew me solely from my online presence, and they cared about my voice in times when it felt like my "real" life didn't. There was camaraderie to our graduating class of internet misfits. We spent a lot of time "curating" (a word that has now become somewhat of a parody in itself) what mattered to us on free platforms. Those platforms were bastions of creativity with music, fashion, art, and free-form thoughts in their purest form. First, the audience listened. Then, of course, the brands—and the dollars—followed.

So I modeled my business on this media trend. It was a gamble that paid off, and a model that needs, to this day, constant revitalization. If we go back to that checklist of burning questions, I can show my work like on a test.

✦ What can I do differently from others?
   I work fast and efficiently. I can wear creative, logistical, and strategic hats. I can delegate. I have a list of business ideas and business names in the top drawer of my desk. I am committed to working hard on something that is mine and that isn't mine. I want to make an impact and am driven to do so.

+ What does currently not exist that would serve a specific need?

Effective word-of-mouth marketing for the social media generation. Events that are designed to be photographed and shared on social. Encouraging brands and commerce through social media and my blogger darlings.

+ What is an open arena to make money? How are people *not* capitalizing on something?

Brands are trying to figure out their digital strategies, and social media platforms are competing for that same mindshare. There is an opportunity to drive commerce, experiences, and affinity for brands through social media and influential voices as a proxy.

+ What are some characteristics that are unique to me, and how can I manifest those in my business?

I am always looking for people, products, and brands to support. I share what I like with the world, and I have a community of influential friends who are doing the same. I have the experience as a blogger and as a businesswoman to know that there is money on the table and big wins for brands.

+ What is my point of view on said specific industry, and how is it different from others?

I believe women are powerful. I believe that you don't need to fit into a preexisting archetype to have a voice. I believe in the power of community to sell ideas. I believe collaboration can breed creativity and garner attention from unlikely places. The internet has democratized media, and it's now in our hands. More importantly, I see bloggers selling out products, I see people clicking on their products, and I don't see anyone brokering these deals effectively.

✦ How can I achieve my goals authentically, creatively, efficiently, and effectively while maintaining what makes me unique?

Partner with smart people and smart companies. Leverage the support of like-minded businesses. Propel my business further through the use of community and strategic partnerships. Find employees who are hungry and make them give a damn. Do things differently. Know my value prop and what differentiates me from my competitors, a.k.a. my secret sauce.

With this new imagining of the business and where we were going, Serious Business Venture 1.0 pivoted from social media community management, which had been profitable and manageable when it was just Facebook and Twitter but had become time-consuming and money-draining when the number of platforms nearly tripled and video became a demand. We pivoted to being the go-to influencer marketing and events agency.

How did we become "go-to"? Simple, I called us the "go-to agency," and said it over and over again until people believed it (or at least thought it). I wanted my team of twenty-somethings, all fresh out of college and eager to build their résumés, to be able to say with confidence what our company offered and what made it special. I needed to imprint on them my passion with the hope it was contagious and to lead them with the sort of confidence that didn't let on that I was only five years their senior and winging it.

The confidence department is where our male counterparts seem to have the upper hand. There is a thin line between a flat-out lie and projecting confidence in yourself and your team. I always think of my first boss, Curtis, and how his sales-y and exaggerated persona got us in the right rooms and brought us the big business. The golden rule, I determined, was to 100 percent never, ever lie about clients I worked with, capabilities I was actually capable of, or bandwidth. But getting your foot in the door, in any circumstance but especially as a woman, is very hard. We don't get the luxury of chances. When you're putting everything on the line, you need to make your own opportunities.

Sometimes that comes with exaggerations and an oversell (a.k.a. saying yes and figuring it out later). Can you bend the truth about the number of employees you have? Sure, because once you get the money you can hire a team of experts. You can tell a white lie about your office space (holler at a freelancer at home!). And you can certainly pretend to be your own publicist (publicist@yourcompany .com). At its heart, any truth stretching is all about intention. If you exaggerate for the purpose of proving your value, then I consider that a strategic power play. Or at least that's my personal philosophy.

So, as I continued to build out Serious Business Venture 1.0 sans Amanda, if I was preaching that we were the go-to agency, I needed my employees to be my megaphones in their own communities, too. My confidence gave them confidence, leading to a period of momentum that was both powerful and intoxicating.

On one occasion, I hired a group of my friends (literally any friend) to sit at desks in the office, on their laptops, and pretend they were working to help instill confidence in a new client that a "team" was working on their project, not just three of us. (To this day I still think that's a baller move.) I was definitely projecting a false confidence but again: *Confidence begets confidence.* To get on that gravy train, sometimes you just have to spend a little money on enhancing your image and creating your own reputation and then, of course, delivering on that message. Smoke and mirrors is not always a bad thing as long as you're willing to take a long hard look in your own mirror (i.e., at your own reputation—remember that your reputation is your résumé).

Strategic partnerships, blogger outreach, and special events were the whitespace we took over. I became obsessive about new business, going to events four or five nights a week to just talk about the company, see what people were doing, and, more importantly, take note on what they were doing wrong. I know that last nugget sounds harsh, but it's important market research. You have to compartmentalize the emotional aspects of your business and objectively pay attention to other people's, even friends', mistakes to understand the edge that gives your vision. You know what they say: "Don't hate the player, hate the game." It applies to capitalism, too, ladies.

I went out in the hopes of making solid connections or friends in the know. And slowly it paid off, and we signed a number of fashion, lifestyle, and tech companies. People were responding to the niche opportunity we were infiltrating—in addition to my flagrant claim that we were the "go-to agency."

Much of my upswing in the Comeback Year had to do with this blogger community. Clients started to hire my team because of my ties to my IRL internet friends and the word-of-mouth marketing we could execute by just phoning a friend. We traded brand posts for favors or pleases and thank-yous, and my talented connections would often help us out and post for free and even without contracts.

We made magic out of budgets that I would balk at now, but part of solidifying your whitespace's value is to make it cheap and effective. At first. Fun fact: One of the most successful brand events we ever threw was in the Hollywood Hills, at a certain famous heiress's home, for $5,000. I figured that if you can barter for the booze and food, your biggest expenses will be the house rental and valet, which is where relationships come into play. Bartering for services, experiences, or resources can create opportunities and publicity for your contacts and ally businesses. In this sense, creating community is also extremely financially valuable. Hip hip hooray for reciprocity!

For this particular event, I left no stone unturned and no contact unaddressed. I begged a hunky furniture maker to supply us with custom pieces to decorate the house in exchange for some signage around items for sale. I got a new cocktail catering service to donate a full bar in exchange for including their name in the event invite. I somehow got the head chef of LA's cult-famous hole-in-the-wall Thai joint, Jitlada, to come prepare her legendary dishes IRL. (Don't ask me how, I still don't know, but the lesson is you never know until you ask!) We had a champagne-pong table, a chalk artist, and a glassblower stationed in different areas of the heiress's home.

Put aside for a second the fact that there will always be kinks. As it turns out, floating candles in a pool might light the plastic filtration system on fire, which I effortlessly put out while simultaneously freaking out. A cleaning crew is a critical part of catering, but before I learned this lesson, I ended up scrubbing dishes in my stilettos. It was the most chaotic event I have thrown to date, but it's also my best case study for how far relationships and the barter system can extend a tiny budget.

Not to mention, it was a simpler landscape, one where influencers posted about the shit they actually believed in and why. There were no Federal Trade Commission–mandated hashtags or required post copy or multiple levels of approvals. Were they the good old days? Sort of. Not to get sappy, but a group of fashion-savvy women were amplifying their voices on their own terms. OG word-of-mouth marketing was becoming a mega-effective landscape for the right brands or partnerships. It worked for one reason and one reason only.

Hint: I'm talking about a word listed in the previous four burning questions.

Bonus points if you can guess what it is. Likely you've heard it time and time again.

"Authentic."

How can you *authentically* meet your goals? If you are running a business, be an unrelenting part of the community behind it. If you run a donut shop, you better freakin' LOVE DONUTS, and you better be partnering with the Better Donut Bureau to bring your donut creations to the masses. You better be organizing donut tastings and meeting with new potential donut distributors on the regular and basically never be not thinking about donuts. (I think you get the point and, also, I really wish this was a real thing.)

The donut example is my attempt to cutely drive home this very real concept: My success in my first business came from being a part of the conversation and the community I was serving. When the dollars rolled in, I made sure my friends got paid, often much more than what I was making at the time. When building a business and starting out, you have to ask for a lot of favors. Some people will help you and others won't. The people who help you will often be the game-changers for your entire business trajectory, and I am so freaking thankful for the women I came across during the Comeback Year. The women who sent intro emails trusting I would deliver, the women who threw my hat in the ring for a new business pitch, the women who told someone that they "*had* to work with" me. I remember every favor. (This is not to say that men didn't support my come up, because a handful absolutely did, but women can and should bring a respect and reciprocity to the game.) We understand the power of cosigning each other, which is at the root of what a WorkParty is: that we can do this and we can do it together. We lean into our power, we figure out how to work the corporate system as best we can, we demand equality, but we are here now in a place where the power and possibility are within reach, so let's grab and make it our own, on our terms and, most importantly, together.

The support from these women gave way to my biggest lightbulb idea and a business that would shape the next big chapter of my life. The idea that collaboration with women is stronger than competition with them is the nugget of gold that launched Create & Cultivate.

During Serious Business Venture 1.0, I kept Some Notes on Napkins happy and healthy and well-fed with a consistent amount of content. Like the little blog that could, it allowed me to leverage my role as a member of the media to get into events, onto panels, and in people's newsfeeds. Sometimes this involved a sponsored post for a deodorant brand or a new mascara, but more often than not, I posted outfit flat lays, playlists, and design inspiration, rarely getting on the other side of the camera.

I simultaneously emphasized to my team that we should treat our company as a client, devoting resources and a marketing push behind our own brand. We maintained a weekly newsletter spotlighting stuff we loved, curated with lifestyle goods, tech innovations, events, and companies we aspired to work with. This goes back to the whitespace checklist, because once you've established who you are, you have to market the marketing. The brands of today are media companies, publishers, and storytellers, and you have to tell that story to keep people engaged. Paying attention to trends and aesthetics and community building is critical. Community can make all the difference in attracting the ideal talent and the ideal clients.

I promise you will have an identity crisis and you will rebrand everything more than once, but the important thing is to iterate with your business and continue to define it on your own terms. Iterating, much like pitching, is a skill that takes practice—not every pivot or turn you make will be the right one, and you might have to throw that shit in reverse occasionally. But if you don't constantly try new approaches, you won't know which one is the optimal route.

In the spirit of leading by example, I want to shout out a few other female-led companies that not only found their whitespace, but made waves doing it. I personally know the majority of these gals, and I want to make sure the whitespace credit is given where it's due.

1. Away
Helmed by Jen Rubio and Stephanie Korey, this VC-funded luggage company revolutionized travel for busy entrepreneurs. Their suitcases are mostly known for their built-in phone-charging outlet, chic branding, and in-house magazine, *Here*. But I know these women as former Warby Parker executives, some of the first people and brands to sponsor Create & Cultivate. I see women who practice what they preach and invest in other women. I, in turn, invested in their company. If we want more boss babes at the top, let's start funding their visions where and when we can.

2. Outdoor Voices
Austin native Tyler Haney founded her activewear line when she was still a student. By the time this book comes out, she won't even be thirty. Good ideas do not discriminate against age, and Tyler is a good example of someone who didn't let preconceived notions of being "too young" stop her. She tapped into the growing athleisure market, but came at it from a new angle: Make it human. Don't just target the athletes or the yogis. Aim to inspire the everyday active person, the "hiking buddy that brought the snacks," as Tyler has adorably said in past interviews. She also secured major dollars in investment from the one and only A.P.C., which is pretty validating in its own right.

3. Framebridge

Susan Tynan launched a business based off a human insight (read: complaint) that most young adults are initially shocked by: It's expensive as hell to frame art. It's a right turn from her early career at the White House (impressive), but it paid off. Susan has made art and design more accessible for young people, and reimagined what used to be a pretty painful consumer process.

4. S'well

Founded by boss babe Sarah Kauss, S'well was the fast-growing women-owned business in 2015 in America. The stainless steel water bottle collection has become a staple for entrepreneurs on the go who want to keep their hot liquids hot and their cool liquids cool. The partnerships she has executed are bananas, from Starbucks to Swarovski, and she's only getting started. I love that an idea as straightforward as a water bottle can tap into the zeitgeist so efficiently.

5. Spanx

Oh, Spanx. The brand that needs no introduction. My first pair of Spanx became my secret weapon, my best friend, and my mortal enemy. I'm sure founder Sara Blakely understands the nuanced relationship consumers have with her tummy-tucking intimates line. But that hasn't stopped us from buying these magic body-shaping undergarments, and collectively, we have helped Sara become a billionaire—yes, with a *B*. And if there's one thing I love more than taking my Spanx off at the end of a long night, it's seeing women in the billion-dollar boys' club.

6. Carol's Daughter

Lisa Price has set the gold standard for the African-American hair care game. She's been cosigned by Oprah and invested in by Jay-Z and Will and Jada Pinkett Smith, just to name-drop a few. She sold her company to L'Oréal and faced some backlash from her community for "selling out," a concept that many entrepreneurs battle with. She has spoken about rewriting the narrative that people (read: haters) had assigned to her, which upset a small portion of consumers. She's a champion of positivity and a woman I look up to.

7. *The Mis-Adventures of Awkward Black Girl*

Issa Rae is my number one girl crush, and I'm not afraid to admit it. Part of what I love about her is that she started by starting. She put out *Awkward Black Girl* on YouTube, made use of a free storytelling platform, and committed to it. There was no half-assing or "eventually" in her world. She worked hard on a story that she had stake in, and it was the stepping-stone to her smash-hit HBO series, *Insecure*.

Whitespace is important as hell. Sadly, starting a business isn't as comfortable as hotel bedding or a fresh pile of warm laundry. But *every idea is worth nurturing if you believe in it*. I've started four different companies. Spoiler alert: They aren't all here today. And I didn't know what potential any of them had until I took the leap. I'm not a religious person, nor have I ever been confused for a hopeless romantic. I'm a realist who has pulled all-nighters trying to make businesses that matter and a human woman who has cried herself to sleep many a night. You don't have to know exactly what your brand or business or idea will turn into; you just have to try it and build it until it has its own DNA and demand. It's more doable than people (read: the patriarchy) let you believe.

The best advice, though? Start by starting.

The Real Real

The Comeback Year couldn't have happened if it weren't fueled by a year of personal turmoil. I'm sure that sounds clichéd or dramatic, but it's an absolute truth. Remember: You are your failures—in the most empowering way possible.

And when things get bad, there's a point where it doesn't get worse. Classically trained SMART people like Malcolm Gladwell could probably articulate this like an economic principle meets sociology theory and dub it something like "The Law of Diminishing Shittyness," but I cannot do that for you. I can just say, as straightforwardly as I can, that when everything seems to crumble around you, it eventually can't crumble anymore. And then things slowly start to get better. You start to get better. You start becoming a human again. Be kind to yourself and be proactive about your healing. Prioritize your sanity one mantra, journal entry, yoga class, or glass of wine at a time. During the portion of my first year in LA when I got dumped by my long-term boyfriend, a friend very seriously looked at me (while I was crying) and said, "No offense, but who fucking cares."

The thought startled me because, well, she was right. People get dumped every day. Shitty things happen. I followed up her remark with, "I just wish good things happened to good people." To which she responded, "I don't know, Jackie, babies get cancer." And there it was, the truth. Horrible, gut-punching, hard-to-process things happen to good people every single day. Conversely, great things happen to bad people all the time. You will get dumped, and life will be hard AF, and guess what? You will move on, no matter how impossible it feels. It was a harsh but eye-opening way of reminding me that there is beauty and comfort in the shared human experience.

That should be a teaching moment for all of you. Your career, your job, that one bad meeting, it doesn't make you. It certainly won't break you. And when you're seriously stuck in the mucky muck of it, stop thinking about yourself for one second.

That said, I am really proud of how I crawled out of a very horrible, no good year. I came out of it and was still vulnerable and emotional when I could have easily become hardened and bitter. I was able to accidentally launch the 2.0 version of my business and myself simultaneously. I found that women wanted a place to talk real talk— *I* wanted a place to talk real talk about being a business owner and about being a woman in business. My peers were seeking the same advice I was. I wanted women to have a space in which to connect with one another about being entrepreneurs. The good, the bad, and the ugly.

So there you have it. While my first business partnership wasn't the sweeping success I'd hoped for, it taught me everything I needed to move on and succeed. That's the good thing about messes: They get cleaned up, and you come out the other side smarter and wiser, if a little dirtier.

I'm 90 percent confident that I can identify the elements that grew me as a person and an entrepreneur that year, and I hope I was able to boil down the chaos of it all into a few concrete, actionable lessons for you. But it would be remiss of me not to think that at least 10 percent of the Comeback Year was luck and magic that I can only marvel at and be grateful for. Maybe that was luck and magic that I had unknowingly created for myself or invited into my life. The late great film producer Samuel Goldwyn has a quote that I come back to often: "The harder I work, the luckier I get." I agree.

So that's it. Work hard, stay in the game, and trust that you're laying the foundation for your own future luck.

chapter five

The Ah-Ha Moment

It's only years into Create & Cultivate that I'm starting to understand why they call it an "ah-ha" moment.

When the idea strikes, there is a moment of zen, as Jon Stewart would say (although, TBH, I don't meditate—here's to 2019 New Year's resolutions). Anyway, the idea moment is this euphoric "ahhhhhhh." Kind of like a release into the universe, where everything—missteps, mishaps, mistakes—feels peaceful and makes sense.

And then, a moment of laughter: a quick HA! Because you think, *That can't be it! That is crazy.* The ah-ha moment is much more manic than most people think. It's a series of moments where you "ah" and then "ha" over the course of many weeks, many months, and then many years. The sexy story the media loves is that the golden idea happens in an instant. You're strutting down the street, earbuds in, when all of the sudden, the lightbulb moment hits. The world stops moving all around you. You've figured out the secret! Truthfully, though, the ah-ha moment is much more anticlimactic. It's nothing like Christmas morning as a kid. Nothing like a first kiss.

Far from it. At nearly every step of the way while launching a business, you question the legitimacy of what you're thinking and doing, but you are propelled forward at such speed. You're wondering, *Am I insane?* Which, if you're starting a biz, you are. Anyone who wants to be an entrepreneur is definitely a little insane. But never let that stop you.

So the big question is: How do you go from the "ah" to the "ha" to create a business? It's pretty simple, really: You start.

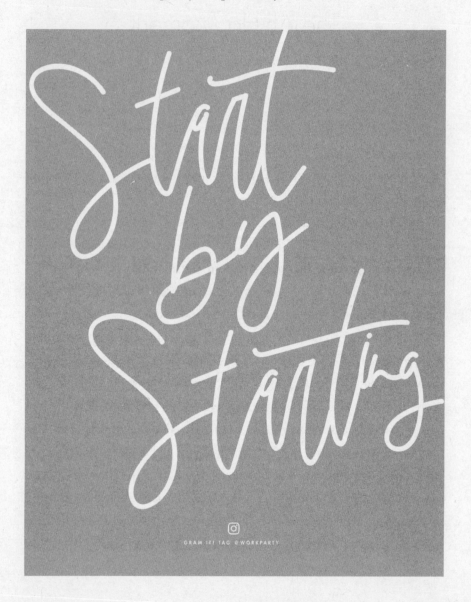

Take Your Creative Projects Seriously

In the last five years I've had the privilege to meet so many women who are working full-time jobs and "side hustling" on their creative projects or passions. And they take that word "hustle" very seriously. But before we talk about hustle, let's chat for a minute about taking your creative projects seriously. What does that even really mean? Are you a part-time crochet genius and a full-time marketing exec? But how do you decide that it's time to go crochet all the way?

Here are four incredibly important questions you need to ask yourself when thinking of moving your side hustle into the spot-light:

1. Does my product already exist?
Subquestion: Is there a reason that it doesn't exist?

Think about the validity of your idea and its true market value. Whether it's a physical product or, just for instance, a women's conference, does your idea/product make the market and the world a better place? Do your research. Look into patents filed, scour the internet—see if someone HAS tried it before. Find out all the reasons it didn't work for them. You could even be so bold as to call that person up! Send them an email and talk to them about why they failed. Fortune favors the bold.

2. Am I offering the market a better version of something that does exist?
Subquestion: If I'm really honest, is it really, truly better?

If the product exists in some form, you would be wise to get a second opinion here—an honest, trusted friend, family member, or confidant who can give you, *hopefully*, an unbiased opinion about your business idea. Fortune also favors the honest.

3. Am I willing to lose everything?

Subquestion: Am I ready to gain everything?

Success is two-sided. Alli Webb of Drybar put her and her husband's life savings ($50K) into the first location. The cofounders of Tone It Up took $3K and built their multimillion-dollar business. Jeni Britton Bauer lived out of her car when she launched her first ice cream business, which, you should note, did not succeed. These women were willing to risk it all. That's what being an entrepreneur means. Now the subquestion about "gaining everything" isn't about money, really. It's about incremental gains. The tiny wins, the late nights, the early mornings, eating your words because you fucked up and also skipped lunch that over time add up to make a business.

You will not gain everything overnight. Hollywood loves the term "breakout star," but every single breakout star has been steadfastly working for years. For instance, 2017 was the year of Tiffany Haddish. The actress, who became the first black woman comedian to host *SNL* in its over forty-year run (yes, seriously), had been performing at the Comedy Club since she was a teen. She also talks openly about living out of her car at one point. (And you should read her book—it's amazing.) Success takes a long time, and a lot of little things coming together.

But what are *you* willing to risk in order to win?

4. Is it all you can think about?

This one is simple: If it's all you can think about, it's time to give it a go. *

---

*One more important question: *Do you have the money to do this?* Have you been able to save enough money to get you through the first six months without drawing an income? Capital is often a barrier to entry that holds many women back, and I'd be remiss if I didn't point out that some of the women I mention in this book had outside help. Alli Webb risked her life savings, but she also had a successful brother who was willing to finance her idea. Rebecca Minkoff had a plan B of working for her father, and her brother, like Alli's, helped fund the early stages of her eponymous company. Not everyone has this luxury or a family member who is willing to take out a second mortgage on their home.

Now, let's chat side-hustle specifics.

Ellen Bennett, of Hedley & Bennett, launched her apron business while working full-time as a line cook. What started out in her living room as a one-woman operation has, over the course of three years, exploded into a 14,000-square-foot factory and showroom outfitting more than four thousand restaurants worldwide. In the early days, Bennett was scrappy (and she still is). She peddled her aprons at the local farmers' market every weekend and barged her way into some of the best-known culinary establishments uninvited. "I didn't let anything get in my way. If I fell, I picked myself up again and kept going. I learned something new every day and worked through every challenge. It wasn't easy, but if you persist, anything is possible." After two years of side hustling while cooking up a storm in kitchens, she finally quit her job to grow Hedley & Bennett, which she started without any outside funding and has grown into a multimillion-dollar business.

Daina Trout, cofounder and CEO of the kombucha company Health-Ade, was working high up at a pharmaceutical company, coming home in tears every night and wondering what her next move was. Though she was "moving up the corporate ladder and doing pretty well," she told me, "I'm somebody who doesn't even take Tylenol. So to work for a pharmaceutical company was weird. I was a number. It was very *red-tapey*, and I was particularly rebellious. There were a hundred thousand employees there, and I wanted to be a leader. I felt like I had it in me to do that."

For about four months over the summer of 2012, Trout and her two other cofounders tried working the farmers' market circuit on nights and weekends while keeping on with their day jobs. "I was completely driving myself into a brick wall," she said. Right around November 2012, the trio knew they couldn't continue at this pace, nor were they doing well at either job. They weren't going to expand, "certainly not into Whole Foods," Trout shared, if they didn't commit. So in December they shook hands, made a pact, and as of January 1, 2013, they were full-time Health-Ade. "I remember that first day we showed up, January first, and realized, 'Oh shit, there is no paycheck coming. And we have no money.' Maybe six hundred dollars. It was really dumb in a lot of ways, when you look back at it on paper."

Now, you don't have to launch in a farmers' market to be successful. But you do have to be willing, like these women were, to put almost everything on the line.

––––––––––––

Around the time of my Comeback Year, the first rumblings of Create & Cultivate were starting to build in the back of my mind. I knew that I wanted to get together women who were having similar struggles to what I had just gone through, but even after a Google deep dive, I couldn't find the community I was seeking. (See question number 1: Does my product already exist?) I was looking for something that not only spoke to me, but also felt familiar (a.k.a. not a cold, generic page talking about the legal minutiae of breaking up with a business partner or a Yahoo! Answers forum). I wanted answers to my questions that felt authentic to my situation (hell, my generation!) and that community just didn't exist.

My questions were about launching, hiring, firing, what to charge, how to charge, how to find clients, how to get clients to actually pay, raising money, sexist remarks, ageism rearing its ugly head, not being taken seriously . . . the list went on. And it still goes on—I have questions to this day. That's why I knew it needed to exist no matter what. (See question number 3: Am I willing to lose everything?)

However, beyond the business of *the business*, the most important question I had was "Why?" Why do I feel compelled to do this? And what purpose will it serve—besides giving me comfort and crowd-

sourced counseling? (See question number 4: Is it all you can think about?)

To be honest, I wasn't thinking bigger picture. Create & Cultivate mostly grew out of selfish reasons—I felt isolated and alone post biz-partner breakup, and I wanted that squad and that sense of cama- raderie. I also wanted *and felt compelled* to be vulnerable about my ex- perience. The shame of the situation was starting to wear off, and when I spoke about my story, people were relating right back their own setback stories and mistakes made. There was a movement here a-brewing, I could feel it.

Of course, conferences existed before Create & Cultivate—I had been to them, met great people, made some rad connections—but I don't remember ever leaving feeling *inspired*. (See question number 2: Am I offering the market a better version of something that does exist?) I wanted to feel inspired, and I wanted to feel that way sur- rounded by other powerful women talking about real-life problems versus glossing over them with semantics and niceties. There were college alumni association mixers, which always felt a bit sad and gra- tuitous, more like a #humblebrag reunion for people showing you how far they've come instead of genuinely connecting and wanting to lend a hand. There was no vulnerability, just big-box production and thou- sands of people in an arena or sad conference rooms and awkward handshakes.

It was all very, to be blunt, dull. There was nothing compelling about the conferences that were already available; typically atten- dance was mandated and the experience was not exciting. There cer- tainly weren't Instagrammable moments. Def not. Think "Hello, My Name Is" stickers and fifty shades of beige. Hotels with drab carpet, gross food, and bad lighting. Information drolly doled out by people who, even if they had the business acumen, didn't "get" what millen- nials wanted or needed to hear.

First thing, I knew that Create & Cultivate needed to be visually stimulating. Everything was moving online, sure. But that meant there was a massive opportunity to create an online experience IRL. Online hasn't eviscerated the offline experience, as some have cautioned. Rather it's made real life all the more important.

What I set out to create was something that looked like me, felt like me, and spoke *to* me. I had built a marketing brand for Serious Business Venture 1.0 around style and design, but it was always for my clients. Now I was in the driver's seat, building experiences and buzz for my own idea. I was becoming my own client. So I did what every new entrepreneur does: I got the domain, trademark, and Instagram handle and just started putting it out there, projecting a brand presence I liked and hoped others did, too. (See addendum question: Did I have the money? Yes. I bootstrapped Create & Cultivate. Bootstrapping means launching and growing without any external capital or investment. It started out small. It gradually grew. Plus, I still had money coming in from my first company and from the blog. It wasn't much, but it was enough to make it work.)

It was on.

When I say Create & Cultivate started out small, I mean it. Not Harry Potter living-under-the-stairs small, but close to it when you compare the scope of Then to Now.

It took three years of doing this and not making money (in fact, losing some) before I realized this might be something worth investing time and money into. Keep in mind I was still running the not-so-little Serious Business Venture 1.0 that could.

Create & Cultivate wasn't fully formed . . . yet. I hadn't quite nailed down the point or the branding . . . yet.

In the beginning, the single most important meeting you take is with yourself. Not with a friend or an investor. Not a VC who says, "Yes! We want to give you seventeen million dollars to launch." No. It's you. If you're honest, you will learn more about yourself when starting a business than you would ever know otherwise.

At this point in my career, thanks to past missteps and misfortunes, I knew what I wanted and what I didn't. I had been burned, but it wasn't so bad that I couldn't recover. Rule number one of entrepreneurship? Resiliency required.

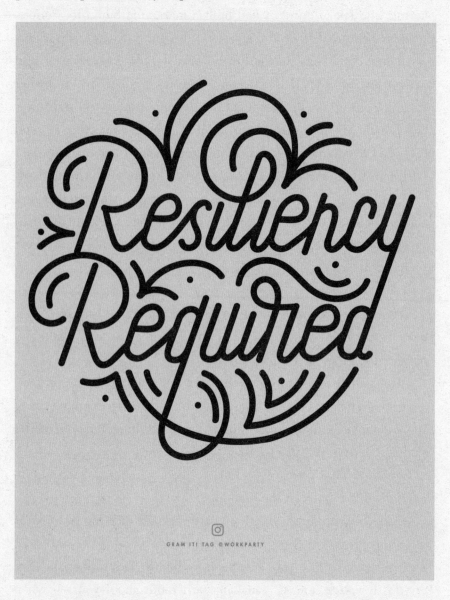

GRAM IT! TAG @WORKPARTY

So what knowledge was I bringing to the table? When starting Create & Cultivate, I knew that I didn't want to do it solo. I didn't necessarily want another business partner, in the same way that you don't necessarily want to jump into a relationship after a real shit-kicker. But I wanted a tribe of women. I needed women IRL . . . I wanted women I could text at 2 a.m. who I knew were also up burning the early-morning oil. Screw midnight—we work past midnight! I wanted us to be able to grease our wheels together and get those wheels rolling.

Create & Cultivate wasn't my first idea. It wasn't my first business. I had no idea if it would make money or if there would be an audience, and yet I took Create & Cultivate very seriously from the jump. Whitespace + momentum = I knew I had to capitalize on the idea. And while it wasn't necessarily my first idea or my best idea, it's the one that hit. If your idea is fueled purely on passion and drive, that's probably the venture that will eventually surprise you.

That doesn't mean it's going to come easy. Or fast. While the Create & Cultivate trajectory looks like it's been fast and furious, it is the hardest I've ever worked. It's also the happiest (#workparty) I've ever been in my career. There were the countless late nights. I got involved in the intimate details (still do), from every complaint to glowing review. People would write asking "When's the next one?!" and others would write and say it let them down, that they wished they had received harder, more concrete business advice. As such, we made it a priority to not leave anything up to chance. Our editor-in-chief fine-tooth curates the content that happens the day of the conference. Every question that gets asked onstage has been vetted through her to ensure that attendees have the best time and receive the advice they're looking for. No detail is overlooked.

And I still get involved with iteration after iteration of design to make sure everything is freaking amazing from the moment an attendee walks in the door.

If you've not yet experienced a Create & Cultivate conference, I'll walk you through the magic. On the day of the conference, registration opens at 8 a.m. Attendees arrive dressed to IMPRESS. They line up early. Their heels are high, and so are their expectations. Once inside the space, they are greeted by meticulously curated Instagrammable moments built to inspire, whether that means a massive pink neon sign that reads "Collaboration over Competition," or a donut wall (we were the first!). There are carefully orchestrated sitting areas with beautiful furniture, all hand-selected. Our decal game is strong. There are VIP lounges, beauty lounges, and a pop-up market filled with everything a woman might need—from advice on how to build your Squarespace site to a mani-pedi cab for a quick touch-up. We run two stages simultaneously that service Track 1 and Track 2, one track that focuses on entrepreneurship and the other on building your brand. The two-track system came about as the result of attendee feedback. There were attendees who wanted panels with more entrepreneur-focused information and those who wanted more content/blogger-focused info. We aim to please.

Over the course of the day, we run about six panels per stage. Topics vary from conference to conference, but we talk startup life 101, financing, growing your followers, how to make it in the beauty biz, what it's like to be a female CEO, and why diversity and inclusion are important at the top. We keep it professional on panels, but we don't play it safe. We keep it real. In the middle of the day comes Mentor Power Hour, when attendees meet with two preselected mentors for thirty minutes each in a group of about fifteen. It's one of the most hands-on and important aspects of the Create & Cultivate experience, and is often noted by attendees as an incredible value add because they get to ask direct questions to the women they admire most. And they get direct answers. And, of course, throughout the day there are loads of food, coffee, and snacks. And usually right before everyone joins together at the main stage for the keynotes, we cheers to wins, successes, new friends, and potential business ops.

Then comes the pop-off: the keynotes.

As I write this, over five years from those initial thoughts, Create & Cultivate is bigger than I could have ever imagined. On September 9, 2017, we hosted a conference on the Microsoft campus featuring keynotes by Issa Rae, Mandy Moore, Brooklyn Decker, and more. The day before, I'd traveled up two elevators, down corridors, on what felt like a secret mission to meet Microsoft CEO Satya Nadella. He shook my hand and thanked Create & Cultivate for the work it is doing.

At Create & Cultivate Seattle, Issa Rae danced out onto our main stage to Kendrick Lamar's "Humble" as the crowd roared, danced, and cheered—a thousand women eager to be inspired. We talked about failure: "I can't go a day without failing. I think where I thrive is knowing I'm not gonna make that mistake the same way again," she said. We talked about female friendships: "I love women. Some of my best friends are women," she joked. "There's just a comfort and a shorthand and a support system. There's a narrative that we don't support each other, that we're catty, that we tear each other down. That's never been my experience. It's so rewarding to grow with so many different women." And we talked about changing the boys' club: "You're constantly getting excuses from higher-ups that they can't find people . . . But they're not trying hard enough," she said onstage to an enraptured crowd. "Sometimes you have to take a risk on people that have no experience, so they can work. For us it was making sure that we're doing our part to give other people the spotlight."

She sent me a thank-you note afterward. Yes, Issa Rae, the woman hailed as bringing truth to television and a voice to women of color, sent me a thank-you note. If that's not a "WTF, pinch me" moment, I don't know what is. These aren't moments you can dream up because they are so much bigger than your dream. There have been so many "pinch me" moments like these along the way. If you're reading this thinking, *This is the opposite of "sit down, be humble,"* you're not entirely wrong. These are the BIG moments, the ones you tell your grandchildren about.

There are two reasons I bring up these big moments: For every instance that seems too big, too unreal, know I moved to LA not knowing a single person, I cried on my floor for many months, I relentlessly failed, I had no business plan and no connections. My point is you can do this. You should *dream BIG*. I was a human with a laptop and a ferocious capacity to follow up and put myself out there. I had grown immensely. And yes, I was adding exclamation points to all my emails at this point. Even x's and o's. Why? Because why not!

Know Your Brand and Stick to Your Guns

Let's reverse, though. It wasn't all Issa Rae all the time. Let's time-travel to year one, 2011, when I teamed up with the Ace Hotel to bring creative freelancers together in Palm Springs to talk about business strategies and to network poolside. The fifty-person event, which consisted mostly of people I had a personal connection to and who also happened to be some of LA's best creatives, was basically a micromini version of today's Create & Cultivate conference. I hosted one of the workshops dubbed "Photoshop 101 for Bloggers." There was a DIY shibori tie-dye workshop with lifestyle blogger duo Honestly WTF. And a creatives dinner hosted by Levi's. We had Keep A Breast on-site doing live breast casts and raising money for breast cancer awareness, and there were cocktails and fireside chats where everyone opened up about their work, their insecurities, and what was and wasn't working. After the event, people kept asking, "When's the next one? When's the next one?" It felt like the best parts of summer camp—new friends and fireside confessions—for a new creative class. I started to get a warm and fuzzy kind of feeling. The demand was, quite literally, hitting me in the face.

So was the need to price it appropriately.

So how do you determine ticket pricing or set a value on experience? What's the ROI of something that will last you a lifetime? Original general admission tickets were set at $350. We have yet to change that price, despite the fact that some conferences now cost upwards of $1,500 per ticket. We've had people tell us we're charging way too little. We've also had many attendees tell us that $350 is too expensive for them. We understand both sides of the spectrum. Could we charge more? Probably. But it's so important that we don't alienate our OG fanbase or women to whom $350 is a lot of money. To be frank, it *is* a lot of money, so we consider the value we provide. This isn't about taking dollars from women; it's about building something bigger.

pause

This is a rare occasion where you go with what's working. Go where the momentum is. Because, guess what, you can't manufacture momentum. Even if it's happening in a super unexpected place, you follow it.

The pitch was simple: Create & Cultivate was designed to help women create and cultivate the careers of their dreams. Isn't this what we all want? A career that we're not only proud of at the end of the day but actually have fun pursuing? I know it's what I want. But like we said earlier, dreams without plans tend to fall flat. Again, I had plans, but didn't realize that soon I would be CEO of not one but two companies. The aggressive growth of both would take a toll on me personally and professionally.

Cut to Create & Cultivate, 2013, which was a bit more put together. That conference was hosted at the Standard in Downtown Los Angeles. Again, a group of fifty bloggers, PR mavericks, creatives, and tastemakers (and people I didn't actually know) gathered in the rooftop Biergarten, perched on yellow Tolix chairs, primed and ready to hear from the best in business. On that particular Saturday my team of two and I had rallied speakers and noted bloggers like LEAFtv, Mr. Kate, Jessica Comingore, the Denim Refinery, and executives from Bucketfeet and Warby Parker.

I remember looking around at everyone conversing, exchanging ideas, and shaking new hands. In. Real. Time. It's something I hadn't really seen since moving to LA: the sharing of a narrative, taking the online offline, creating and cultivating.

I started realizing that a majority of the creative people I knew were stuck behind a computer eight hours a day (of which I was 100 percent guilty) and wanted to get a little analog, a disconnect from the digital.

At the time our following wasn't huge, but we had a brand and a social strategy that we believed in, and we used that to carry us through until the numbers grew. We live-tweeted and Instagrammed from the event in order to foster a digital community and scale our reach. We knew the power of a hashtag. Of trending. This was the beginning of what would become the online site and blog. We knew the content in person had to drive to something. And even though Create & Cultivate was pretty, we knew that the content needed to be nittier and grittier. We didn't want to ask what kind of avocado toast women were making, as delicious as it is, because that isn't the whitespace. Women wanted real answers and real vulnerability.

After hitting the road (or sky, I should say), hosting a few more of these in various cities, and taking up residence on friends' couches where I could, I knew I had to sit down and make serious moves. What was this thing that was starting to take up so much of my time? And from my employees' perspective, which company did we work for? Create & Cultivate or the marketing agency? Yikes, the real answer was that I didn't know. I hadn't planned for this moment.

Get Ready to Grow and Iterate

By the time we hosted Create & Cultivate in Chicago in October 2015, we had our shit down. What was once a team of two sweaty (#glowing) gals moonlighting as event producers, coat-checkers, and professional dishwashers was now a well-oiled machine. I had a staff of four, all of whom were "slashies": marketers slash event producers slash florists slash writers slash developers. They understood the hustle and were simultaneously working on their personal brands, something I readily encouraged. Their presence in their communities was bringing more women to our growing platform.

The feedback from our attendees was crucial in our growth and optimization. You can't be afraid to read those one-star reviews, too. I learned from our mistakes in production or amenities or expectation setting and embraced the warm and fuzzy comments that told me that our events had been changing lives.

My life was likewise changing, but it wasn't always warm and fuzzy behind the scenes. For one, I had never thrown an event as large as Chicago, we didn't hire any temp staff to help on-site at the beginning (I didn't even know you could do that), we were literally running laps for forty-eight hours, and by the end of the night our feet would be totally swollen to the point where walking was a legitimate challenge. I hadn't eaten or slept in days. I do remember crying, some happy tears, some straight painful tears. In retrospect I still don't understand how we pulled that off. And today, I always wear sneakers leading up to the moment I hop onstage. (It's a personal choice, but it's important to me to wear cute shoes onstage. I'm someone who thinks it's possible to be feminine, chic, and boss AF. Not to mention, the bigger Create & Cultivate became, the bigger the name I sat across from, and our keynotes often have hair and makeup done before grabbing the mic. I didn't want to be seen as the messy founder. And I didn't want to feel disrespectful. But I also know it's 100 percent impossible to run a conference in heels. Once I'm off the stage, the sneakers go back on. So does the fanny pack.)

What else went wrong? Once, I literally sat with my head in my hands staring at a wall decal that said "Cultivate & Create." We also did not realize Chicago summers are brutally hot and our oh-so-Instagrammable donut wall started melting. That's right. We got one picture and then the donuts started sliding; each one that hit the ground was like a tiny stab in my side. Once our keynote's chair broke halfway through her convo and she had to crowdsource a new one. And a personal favorite: birds pooping on our attendees in an outdoor venue. Oh, and mic feedback, *allll* of the mic feedback. (Disclaimer: To this day, feedback problems remain out of our control.)

Live and learn. It was hard for me, and remains hard, because I want the event to live up to everyone's expectations. When people pay for an experience, you should deliver on your promise. That's why I re-

Cultivate * Create

main embroiled in the tiny details. On decal placement. Yes, I've cried when things don't look the way I envisioned. I'm only human. My staff knows well at this point that I will cry after any event is over. After everything that goes into putting a conference on, we gather, we toast, I make a sappy from-the-heart speech, and then I cry. Every time. Don't be afraid to show your employees your true emotions and how grateful you are.

And then, when it's all said and done, and decals have been peeled from the walls and floors and *any surface we can find*, we keep learning from our mistakes.

Which is why when you make it past those early days, which you will no doubt feel incredibly emotionally tied to, you can't get bogged down thinking about what you started as. If I had, Create & Cultivate would still be a small pop-up event that my parents couldn't describe to their friends. Or maybe it would have crumbled under the pressure of tough feedback.

Those are the moments that teach you that nothing is unfixable. And if you think one wrong decal or deal gone south is going to sink your business, then sorry to be the bearer of bad news, but you're not building a very strong business. If one nasty Instagram comment makes you question your whole plan, you're not in the right business—but let's get real, I have gotten FIRED UP when I have seen people fully plagiarize our work and gone into a tailspin when something went completely wrong. It's so hard to not take it personally, like they are coming after you. I've put blood, sweat, happy and mad-as-hell tears into this company. I've sat at my desk *physically shaking* when I've seen our exact language, language I worked so hard on creating, on someone else's site. To pretend that doesn't bother me would be a lie. But it's also why you have to continue to get out in front of your competitors. Haters can be good motivators if you let them. Freak out and then put one foot in front of the other.

You have to be willing to LISTEN to your community. Feedback, good or bad, is just data, and the power of that data is in your hands. We knew that as a business we had to become more than a DIY retreat with cocktails. Women wanted hard-hitting business advice. They wanted actionable takeaways to build their blog followings, to launch their design businesses. They wanted to know if they needed investors or whether they should form an S-corp or an LLC. They wanted to know about VC meetings and sitting across from tables full of men. They weren't looking for advice on how to "dress for success" or format an introduction email. As a team, we knew we had to start having tough conversations and putting women on panels who didn't have "Pinterest-perfect" stories.

I felt compelled to lift the curtain on the curated Instagram-worthy world. On the picture-perfect blogging world. Life is not a highly stylized "candid" moment! And we were going to dig into the "why" I had asked myself in the beginning: *Why would people pay attention to this? Why would people care? Why am I so compelled to do this?* The answer was there all along, smacking me in the face, even when I was too tired or too distracted to pay attention.

Women were ready to get real. They were ready to talk about money and sexism in business and reality. And that it bites sometimes. It took me a long time to feel comfortable talking about my ups and downs. To talk about Amanda and the crushing failures I've had. The friends who didn't have my back during that tough time. And maybe that's me and my personality quirks, but something tells me that if you've gotten this far into your WorkParty journey, you might have a bit of perfectionist in you, too. It might feel strange to admit that you don't have it all together. But what I realized was that the more I opened up and told my truth and my story, the more women surrounded me.

Imagine that.

And, more importantly, they surrounded Create & Cultivate. Gathering around a common purpose, an empowered ground. We grew our Instagram following by over one hundred thousand between December 2015 and our conference in Atlanta in August 2016. We found our audience by being true to ourselves, but more improbably, our audience found us and they made us better.

I think so many times we get bogged down in "normal." I have to have this job for this long and move up; I need to meet someone and get married; I need to have lots of friends and an interesting Instagram newsfeed and eat well and be skinny and funny, etc., etc. We see other people's milestones. We don't often see their rock bottoms. Occasionally, we get to see both, and those people become dear to us. Shout-out to Ban.do founder Jen Gotch, who is always sharing the struggle. The reality is there is no normal: Make your own path, take risks, be *terrified*, and create your own sense of happiness.

Ask yourself if you're ready to sunset your day job and sunrise your pet project without going broke.

It's the AHHHHH. And then the HA! You better be ready to enjoy them both.

But don't worry, you don't have to do this on your own. You'll find your tribe.

chapter six

Building Your Tribe

When starting a company, running a company, sweatin' it out at a startup, climbing the corporate ladder, and, in general, being a woman in the workplace, you need to find your tribe. And we'd like to rephrase the old adage "Behind every great man, there's a great woman" to "Behind every great woman are great women."

A tribe is the people who are going to help you, as you them, along your career journey. My tribe is small, tight, and specific, but it definitely didn't start out that way. But with terrible times and lessons learned also come the shining stars, the day-one people who love you endlessly, the people who met you at year three and gave you that leg up, and the seeming strangers who champion you along the ride. These are all important members of what will become your inner circle, and while some members will fade in and out, others will play key roles that they might not even realize will completely change your business.

Building your tribe is the result of serendipitous encounters and spending many a night out when you when you really wanted to be in bed binge-watching Netflix and drinking wine. It can be a chance meeting that alters or expedites your career trajectory. For example, at a small meetup I was producing for a client of Serious Business Venture 1.0, I met two very rad and very smart women. It was a happy hour in Downtown LA, sponsored by a fashion brand and put on by yours truly. A pretty standard affair in which twenty to thirty women all put their bravest face on after getting the invite blasted to their email or seeing the flyer on Instagram and got together for champagne-based cocktails. These intimate events, which seem to be a dime a dozen in a big city like New York or Los Angeles, are how I grew my tribe and my support system. Whether it's a store opening, a new collection launch, a "Women in Tech" event, or a director's Q&A, this is where you find your community, out in the world. Obvious, right? You sign up for newsletters, and you follow aspirational, badass women in your city on Twitter, the 'Gram, the good ol' internetz. You sign up for seminars and automatically (read: graciously) accept plus-one status when offered by a peer. Going to events is not a minor chore to check off your "to-do" list; it's an integral part of building your tribe and your career.

Unfortunately, there's no crash course in networking, and if there is, it's probably a pyramid scheme. Going to events is where being an authentic human is your best bet. Chances are, everyone you meet is going to be an authentic human, too.

These two women worked for a very large corporation and came up to me to say, "Our company needs events like this." They wanted to try and get me a meeting with *their* boss. They had no skin in the game other than wanting to bring something that they thought was cool to the corporate behemoth writing their checks. For me, this was an opportunity of a lifetime. Business cards were exchanged, followed by email niceties, and then the real work began. They spent weeks helping me refine my pitch, giving me advice on how to approach certain subjects and how to price my services (hint: way above what I thought I was going to charge).

Cut to that company becoming one of my largest clients at the marketing agency and then one of the biggest sponsors of Create & Cultivate, taking my business to the next level and also providing me with invaluable relationships with people at the top of the company. These women changed the game for me by setting up a meeting, taking a chance on someone whose work they saw and liked.

You can do the same thing. We all can.

Our most valuable asset in the game is each other, building each other up and pushing each other forward, not down. Collaboration over competition, people! (Not the first time you'll hear me shout this from the mountaintops.) But the first step in meeting these game-changers is to go out in your community.

Your community of confidants, mentors, and experts is one of the most important elements in that special sauce that gives your entrepreneurial efforts lifeblood and keeps you sane. After my great business divorce of 2013, I had to rebuild and restructure my community. Many of my contacts, friends, and mentors made their allegiances clear in the months that followed, and as the dust settled, some of those allegiances weren't to me. The fallout of any breakup is hard, but the aftershocks and unexpected tremors hurt the most. People I thought were in my life unconditionally turned out to have conditional clauses; my pain was too much of a problem for them. Professional contacts I thought would continue to support me picked the other side, and there was backlash and wrongful rumors that I had to just let lie . . . Sleeping dogs, right? And still, it was so hard. How could my friends and peers take sides with the very person who had betrayed me?

So yes, I struggled with these seemingly petty politics. It felt like grade school rules were suddenly being enforced on the adult playing field, and that fundamentally didn't feel fair. And here's where everyone's most-hated piece of advice comes in, a phrase that your mom or

grandma or someone may have told you since you were old enough to fight with your sister in the back of the minivan: *Sometimes life isn't fair.*

It wasn't fair that my business breakup had triggered a whole series of mini breakups in the months following. It wasn't fair that she was the catalyst for our legal battles, or that she got to write her own narrative about our breakup and seed that to our once tight-knit friend group. But life's not fair, and you can only control who you are, your actions, and your output.

For anyone out there feeling lonely, I want to reach out from this page and hug you. I want to tell you that friendships are not linear—you are not born into this world with a predetermined number of friends, and life is an exercise in gaining, keeping, and shedding relationships. If you feel alone right now, you won't be forever. Keep going.

I like to think of my tribe as a diverse group of women that fall into the following categories:

+ Ride-or-Dies
  Friends who have nothing to do with your business and no agenda. These are the people who are either (A) related to you (best sister ever, Jessica Bordner!) or (B) have known you so long, they have an archive of real blackmail material.

+ Business BFFs
  Friends who will affect your business and be your peer counsel and your biggest cheerleaders. Oftentimes these women are met on the job, and even more often than that, they'll be from your first or second job. They will be the ones alongside you when you ask for vacation time for the first time, and who confide in you whether they declared a 0 or a 1 on their W-9, because apparently HR "isn't allowed to advise on that." They are the women you first meet when you're Googling how a "deductible"

works, and you'll be a unit as you rise together. They can be met at any stage of your career, and you'll only get better at identifying the good ones with both gal-pal and business potential.*

+ Mentors

The people who have been there, done that. Women who are influential to you, who will speak to you, who will tell you everything will be OK. Sometimes they are former bosses or family friends or people you've stalked at networking events and/or Instagram. They're usually older and can provide invaluable long-term perspective.

+ Employees

The people who get your vision and show up to support it. The people who represent you, your value proposition, and your mission. The people who prove to your clients or partners that you're legitimate. You pay them for their work, and at times it feels like a lot to be responsible for.†

Here's the thing: I think about business a lot. I think about money a lot. That's not a bad thing, but it can be a lot for people who don't speak about margins or marketing as a love language. This is where your ride-or-dies come in! They remind you that there is a big wide world out there, where there is nature, culture, and the outside uni-

---

*I may be biased because I got two (!!) of these.
†You will most likely be an employee for a long time before you have employees. And that is an adjustment in itself. Remember to have empathy for the positions of both manager/boss and employee.

verse that you've heard a whole lot of good things about. Sometimes the most important (and necessary) step to building a business or taking that next step is taking a break. Don't get so in your zone that you don't remember to enjoy the good life, which includes, but is not limited to, wine, fire pits, string lights, friendship, cuddling with dogs, and Netflix. This is where my daily phone calls to my sister come into play, or my Friday hikes to the Griffith Observatory with ride-or-die Courtney. When you're with your ride-or-dies, backyard dinner parties and digital detoxes reign supreme, and you take your head out of your own hyperfocused world.

My newest, and my most favorite, addition to this list is my husband, David. He is my number one ride-or-die—one who came into my life in 2014. (Big up to Tinder for finding the whitespace in online dating and delivering me my main man.) David came into my life around the time Create & Cultivate was a toddler, and he's been an incredible stepparent to my first child.* He created our logos and much of our early collateral pro bono, but he's done it all with a smile on his face despite my being a harsh-as-fuck creative director. He is a talented artist and the first person to tell me to stop talking about quarterly sales figures and event integration when I so clearly need a break. I love him with my whole heart and appreciate that he makes me have boundaries between who I am and what I do. Sometimes those two identities can feel blurred, but David makes things feel all right.†

---

*Dog.

†Before David, there was a string of boyfriends who definitely didn't "get it." In hindsight, my club promoter boyfriend from New York or my first serious talent manager boyfriend in Los Angeles were not going to be my forever ride-or-dies. And I do want to note that I spent the formative years of Create & Cultivate single, very single. My dog, Noah Wiley, named after a certain *ER* actor, and I formed a pretty steady routine of neighborhood walks and binge-watching *Breaking Bad*. I traveled a lot and stopped trying to find Mr. Right after a date got food poisoning and threw up in my apartment (spoiler: he didn't make it to toilet) and never called me again. Somehow, many months later, I was on a date with David. One week later he came to my thirtieth birthday party, met my entire Los Angeles tribe, and we've been together ever since. He's calm, he's a feminist, and he came out of the blue when I least expected it.

Business BFFs are the next important element of my tribe's ecosystem. The thing my first job gave me, aside from a "fight the patriarchy!" mentality, was two best friends. This is not uncommon, especially for women, and there's a reason for that.

There is a lot that college doesn't prepare you for, which means that my first year out of school and on the job was spent figuring out how to respectfully but firmly ask for the resources I needed, how to set expectations, and how to be heard in meetings. The beauty in this tumultuous, Google-search-fueled time is that there were two other women on my team who were also fresh out of school and learning on the go.

Enter business BFFs Alisa Leonard and Kristen Vang. Our love story began in 2008.

The beauty in first-job friendships is that you will be super different but bonded by circumstances. When the men were out hunting and gathering at the dawn of time, we were at home sharing tips for survival and raising children. We literally survived by trading stories, tips, and, essentially, life hacks. And while it sounds ridiculous to compare Monolithic-era human behavior to startup culture, hear me out.

Alisa is an ex-Mormon with a proclivity toward astrophysics, crystals, emotional intelligence, and futurism.

Kristen Vang is a former midwesterner by way of Australia who has an infectious personality and an affinity for media, creative execution, coding, and business modeling. She can absolutely fuck with an Excel spreadsheet formula.

If you drew a Venn diagram of the three of us, especially at our peak "This is who I am now!" phase from that 2008 summer, there wasn't a whole lot of overlap. I was a fast-talking girl from Florida who liked fashion and was hell-bent on doing something different. Yet the three of us became inseparable after meeting at Attention. We may or

may not have had a YouTube show called *I'm Just Sayin'* where we talked about being working women in our twenties in New York. That content may or may not still be available for your viewing pleasure on the World Wide Web. Seek out at your own risk.

I know I'm preaching to the choir about the importance of female friendships and bonds, but these friends are critical for your first job. Because they can, and often do, turn into your business BFFs.

A business BFF is not just a ride-or-die; she is a ride-or-die with the power to impact your career path. She is not just a friend you make at work and call to vent about your shared boss. She is a peer, an ally, a resource, a therapist, and a fellow soldier. She will help you cobble together a recommendation for a client, proofread your email to HR, and validate your power. She will share her résumé and cover letter with you so that you can make sure yours is par for the course, and she will disclose to you what her annual bonus was. She will help you figure out what that scary contract language actually means and will make the call whether you need to go to urgent care for walking pneumonia or if it really is, as your male boss insists, "a bad cold." She does all this for you because you do it for her, a symbiotic relationship.

Together, you can crowdsource the information you need to survive your first year of the "real world," and then start thriving by your second. Your relationship does not stop when one of you moves on from your position. You have been integral to her success, and she to yours, so you stay in touch, share business plans and legal advice, and help each other grow. If you're lucky, your business BFFs will continue to shine and your collective BFF unit will have a serious entrepreneurial halo around it.

I am lucky enough to have found myself with two business BFFs. Our meeting was no coincidence: We were the only employees under the age of twenty-five at the company, we were the only women, and we were tasked with social media—something that the men in our office didn't take quite as seriously as we knew it should be taken. We had caucuses in the bathroom and secret stall meetings, a bonding ritual that helped us persevere in a male-dominated company. We were a united front, and the front line of our battle to be heard and respected was the workplace.

The three of us now own our own companies. Vang is back in Australia, Alisa in Brooklyn, and I hold it down in Los Angeles. We've made it a point to support each other's new business endeavors, invest in each other's companies, review contracts for each other, and travel the world together in an experience we call GFD (Girl Fun Day) because, let's get real, we all need a little GFD.

It can be hard to figure out who to trust when dollars and cents are in the mix. Competition is in the fabric of our society, and there's a subtext that is hard to avoid: Everyone is your competition. But as I've worked on Create & Cultivate, my little corner in a vast socioeconomic landscape, I have come to have a complex relationship with the notion of competition. I've come to champion the idea of collaboration over competition, and I firmly believe that women helping women is critical to this notion of collaboration. Alisa, Vang, and I have always fostered collaboration among our trio. It's the pulse that has kept us close despite distance, and it's why they made me ugly-cry with their speeches at my wedding. We are bonded by our collective growth and the process that has shaped it. I would not be the businesswoman I am today without these women, my business BFFs.

Now, enter the mentors. Because we weren't born knowing it all—something I always remind freelancers who ask me for advice. (Pro tip: If you work for yourself or by yourself, invest 25 percent of your time into continuing your education. If you are going to compete with bigger companies, if you are going to consult for anyone on their business, you need to be investing time into your competitive and institutional knowledge. End rant.)

Mentors are the people who advise on your decisions and serve as a general counsel for business. These are the people who serve as connectors and advisers, sending you introduction emails to new contacts and cautioning you about loopholes in contract clauses. Their anecdotes typically have some sort of sage business wisdom, and they are particular with their schedules. Mentors come in all shapes, sizes, and ages, and they have the power to be a driving force for your business. They are people who want to see you succeed, and who can give you some of the building blocks for growth. They will most likely introduce you to their lawyer, who is another individual you should get close to. They might workshop ideas with you and get coffee with you once a fiscal quarter. Not your day-to-day contact, they are more of a North Star. Aspirational yet attainable, these people push you to be the person you want to see in their eyes.

Now is where I admit something that makes me a little squeamish: I never had a mentor. I have had wise bosses and aspirational peers, but no one who ever sat down with me and helped me roadmap my career. I started Create & Cultivate partially because I wanted access to mentorship and to collaborate with my dream role models in a forum-like environment. If you have access to mentors who speak to you and will give you their time, seize the opportunity.

Once your business or idea or vision starts to become a tangible reality, there are a few other folks that I highly recommend you add to your tribe. These are the folks I wish I had around for the beginning and end of my first company.

In lieu of the traditional mentorship route, I have recently begun working with a handful of strategic advisers. These are the people who have skin in the game, in the form of equity or phantom equity or other financial compensations. They are experts who you could normally never afford to pay, but because of their aforementioned skin in the game, they cosign your vision without the giant out-of-pocket expense. They can provide the right email introductions, the game-changing advice, and the validation needed to take your business to the next level. This is a more formalized relationship than you'd have with a mentor, and you should tap your strategic partners for counsel, well, strategically. The old adage is true: Time is money. And if you have a strategic adviser, make sure you use their time efficiently and effectively. They are not the people you have "general meetings" with. They are the ones who affect your growth.

At this point, you might not take my word when I say I am not anti-business-partner. I may have suffered from PPTSS (Post. Partner. Trust. Stress. Syndrome.), but I don't want that experience to define who I am and how I move forward. I think business partnership is a wonderful thing, and an even more wonderful thing if you can partner with one of your smarty-pants strategic advisers. I've recently had the pleasure of entering into a partnership with said strategic partner for Create & Cultivate, and I'm not exaggerating when I say she has impacted all areas of my life for the better. Turns out, it feels good to trust again. And have the proper paperwork in place.

The other two people who, if added to your tribe, will minimize error are a lawyer and an accountant. I think this is pretty straightforward, but I can tell you from experience, paying your lawyer a few hundred dollars to review a contract will be a hell of a lot cheaper than most mistakes or clerical errors or client loopholes. As far as accountants go, once you reach your version of critical mass, hire someone other than your mom. I may be biased, but JoAnn and I are a much better mother-daughter duo now that she's not both my bookkeeper and my parent.

And then there are employees. It's a complicated and beautiful thing to build a team. So much so that I want to talk about this in depth in the next chapter.

Keep in mind that your tribe will ebb and flow, people will enter and exit, but hopefully you can count on your ride-or-dies and business BFFs as your core support. And you'll know them when you meet them! The people you add to your tribe are the people who you click with instantly or the people whose enthusiasm for life is too contagious. You respect their brains, know-how, aura, and ambition. You want their respect, confidence, and support. You know the old saying "Show me your friends, and I'll show you your future"? Your tribe should always be present and participatory in your daydreams, if not they may just be hindering them.

I wish I could write a love letter to each of the women who have come into my tribe, but I think you guys would miss most of the inside jokes. So for now, I'll leave you with this: You are not defined by what you do for work. Let your friends and lovers remind you of this important distinction over a glass of wine regularly.

chapter seven

You Gotta Pay the Cost to Be the Boss

(But It's Worth It)

The Boss is in charge. The Boss has flexibility. The Boss takes fancy lunch meetings and gets calls from CEOs of other companies. In theory, it's amazing—and it is at times. But the Boss also carries the weight of the company and everyone's salaries, deals with HR and paychecks, keeps the company afloat, and more. And then some. And more.

Because here is the #realtalk about being the boss: Everyone is your friend, and no one is your friend. The ubiquitous "they" tell you not to take it personally, but you will take everything personally, especially when you have a service-based business. As the boss you care more than anyone else ever will. You will assume power you didn't know you had, you will start to make heart-wrenchingly hard decisions in the blink of an eye, you will learn slowly that not everything is going to go as planned and that that is all right. You will learn to take no shit. You will know your worth and demand it. You will make money and lose it, and as a female boss, you will begin to reconcile your femininity with your bossness because culturally you will find out those things do not always go hand in hand.

You've heard it before. You've seen it before. The media does a great job at pandering to fixed cultural norms.

Women are bossy. Men are the boss.

Women are pushy. Men get things done.

Women are shrill. Men are commanding.

Women are nurturing. Men are leaders.

Flip through 2016–2018 media coverage, and you'll be horrified at the sexist coverage.

Let's scroll through some shining "yes, these are real" examples, shall we?

Chicago Tribune: "Wife of a Bears' Lineman Wins a Bronze Medal Today in Rio Olympics."

Her name is Corey Cogdell-Unrein, but sure let's call her a lineman's wife.

At the 2018 Golden Globes, Rita Moreno, who is one of only twelve people in *history* to EGOT, was listed as a "guest" of Norman Lear. Cool stuff!

Google "Hillary Clinton" and see what populates in your query. Pantsuits! Shrill! Hill without makeup!

The way language is coded in media is shocking when you start to pay attention to it. Search "businesswoman" in stock-photo databases. It looks like we're constantly having meltdowns or pains in our uteri. (Seriously, do it. You'll get a good groan-laugh.) Then search "businessman" (just for shits and giggles). Big difference, right?

The good news is the media portrayal of women at the top being bitchy and demanding (*The Devil Wears Prada*) is not *always* accurate.

Women's attitudes about themselves are also changing; we are no longer beholden to a stale cultural narrative. Times have, as the saying goes, changed.

The Bem test is a great example of this. In the 1970s, Sandra Bem developed the Sex Role Inventory to challenge the view that masculinity and femininity were total opposites and that exhibiting "masculine" or "feminine" traits not matching your gender was a sign of poor mental health. Bem believed that it was possible to be both masculine and feminine at the same time. (BTW, she also considered this the healthiest psychological state for humans, regardless of gender.)

According to Hanna Rosin's book *The End of Men: And the Rise of Women*, since the '70s, women have toed further into what were once considered "masculine traits." Women today are more likely to define themselves as assertive, independent, compassionate, self-sufficient, individualistic, and adaptable—all traits that (*ahem, ahem*) research has shown are indispensable to being a great leader and a great BOSS.

The above research doesn't mean that you can't be feminine and a boss. The exact opposite, in fact. It means that being a woman makes you equally, if not more, suited to be a leader than a man, and that's important. That's a mantra you should repeat every single morning. And it's perfectly possible to create synergy between the "two" sides of yourself to be a better boss.

I'll give you some reasoning as to why some of these traits make women better leaders than men with a car analogy. Someone once told me that men and women are very different drivers. Men look far down the road, but don't pay close attention to what's in their periphery. Women don't look as far down the road, but they are taking everything around them into consideration, from blind spots to the speed of the car on their left. I hypothesize that this is exactly how men lead versus women. Women are always on the lookout for what's around them—whether that's team members or opportunities. They look down the road, but not so far down that they lose sight of what's right next to them. Men go for the big play. They look as far down the road as possible, which isn't wrong, but the way we do business is changing. Collaboration, looking out for what's in front, to your right, to your left, and behind you, is vital to success. I'd argue that women are better at this kind of work, which makes them better leaders.

Walking These Shoes to the Bank

I'm not a stiletto boss. I'm not perfectly put together all the time. Ask anyone who's seen me running around on-site on the days leading up to a Create & Cultivate conference. I rock my Nikes and a fanny pack (so I don't lose my phone) and basically spend three days not once looking in the mirror because it's pure adrenaline, pure passion, and pure exhaustion.

But if I take a hard look back at my younger self, this wasn't always the case. For a long time I thought that I had to prioritize looking good. If I was to be taken seriously, I had to be the perfect package at all times. The road to respect for women is difficult AF. Not only do you have to be the smartest, most capable person in the room but also the most desirable, the prettiest, and, oh yeah, likable.

When I was starting out, I giggled and hair-flipped my way into more meetings than I would like to admit. I brushed off blatantly sexist and ageist remarks along the way and pretended not to hear one too many remarks about women's bodies or the way they dressed from male colleagues. I had everything to lose and nothing to gain from pushing back when people said my rates were too high for such a "young girl" or when clients refused to pay for no good reason other than they had "a lot of lawyers, so don't even think about it."

Hell, did I even know a lawyer? Vulnerability can be a bitch, and men can smell it from a mile away. They will also happily prey on that financially, sexually, and emotionally when it comes to business. I wish I could tell you I have all the answers on how to navigate those situations, but it all comes back to one thing: confidence. Or at least faking it.

I'm going to drill this in one more time. Confidence begets confidence begets confidence.

A few long years into my entrepreneurial ventures, I got confident. I knew what I was doing and I had household-name clients to back me up. I had an office and a lawyer (I finally knew one!). And I wasn't putting up with it anymore. What does that mean? Well, let me tell you about "Richard" ('cause he was a dick). Dick repeatedly tried to lowball the retainer I pitched him and begrudgingly signed the contract at the rate I had pitched. Two days into officially hiring us as his marketing agency, Dick started sending manic rapid-fire emails about how we were doing our jobs and why we weren't doing it "fast enough or good enough." I kept talking him off the ledge, showing him results instead of retaliation. People say success is the best revenge, but results are often the best retort.

That is until one day, once again, something wasn't to his liking again, and he very unprofessionally ripped one of my employees a new one. He repeatedly referred to her as "sweetie" in one of the most condescending emails I have ever read over something so minuscule. So petty and unimportant. I'd had it, and I finally had the power and means to tell him so.

So I fired him. I picked up the phone and called to let him know I didn't think we should work together anymore, it wasn't a good fit for us, nor did it seem to be a good fit for him. He was furious. "You're firing me?!" I remember him raging into the phone. Yes, I was firing him. I was being assertive, independent, compassionate (for my employee), self-sufficient, individualistic, and adaptable, and most importantly, I didn't need his money. (Honestly, I did, but I didn't want to get it like this.) This was a pleasure I had never known—taking the power and not apologizing for it. Have you done this before? If so, give yourself a pat on the back, because Fuck. Yes. My. Friend. It's not an easy call to make, and sometimes you aren't in the position to make those kinds of calls, but as one wise person said, "If you don't stand for anything, you'll fall for everything."

This power came from a wellspring of confidence and experience, but it also came from the fact that I had money in the bank and power in practice. What do those things have to do with each other? Well, turns out, a lot.

WOMEN HAVING MONEY AND POWER IS IMPORTANT. It's actually more than important; it's vital.

According to S&P Global Market Intelligence, which tracks the number of women CEOs in top US and European companies, 2016 was the year in which there were more women than ever heading companies in the S&P 500. Though the number of female executives at big companies is still small, it has increased in recent years. In 2016, out of five hundred companies, only twenty-seven had female CEOs. That number is up from 2015, when it was twenty-two. There are also more women in the workforce than ever before. According to the Bureau of Labor Statistics, women make up 73.5 million, or 47 percent of the labor force. That number is way up from 1945's 29 percent! Numbers! Statistics! Proving my point!

Women are working. And they are climbing ranks, but according to a McKinsey report,[*] they are still underrepresented at every level.

---

[*]*Women in the Workplace 2016* (McKinsey & Company and LeanIn.org), https://www.mckinsey.com/business-functions/organization/our-insights/women-in-the-workplace-2016.

MONEY
is power

Women in C-suite positions: 19%

Women in senior vice presidential positions: 24%

Women in vice president positions: 29%

Women in director positions: 33%

Women in managerial positions: 37%

Women in entry-level positions: 46%

If you have nearly 50 percent of your workforce being led by—and their fates determined by—only 20 percent representation, that's a problem.

So because we're talking about being boss, let's be clear on bossness.

There are more women in the workforce than ever before and, as stated above, there are more women holding executive positions at companies. This is important for one major reason: Whether we like it or not, money is power. Money gives you opportunity. It "talks," as they say. The more women we have in positions of power, making or handling money, deciding who that money goes to, the better. We need women hiring women, women giving women that meeting, that chance to build something. That is how we will start seeing real change in the workplace.

Which brings me to a more macro point: Women need to start talking about money and stop hating on other women who are making money. This is also an attitude that I've had to grow into.

About two years ago, I was on the phone with a key editor at a major magazine. The interview had been arranged by my PR company, and I set myself up to be hit with a question I wasn't entirely ready to answer. "Women need to be more comfortable talking about money," I told the editor. "We need to tell each other what we want, what we make, and how we handle salary negotiations. If we don't talk about money," I went on, "we will never make the big moves."

She didn't miss a beat. "So, how much did you make last year?" she asked.

I had to answer. I knew I had to literally put my money where my mouth was. But I was also terrified. This was going into print. Everyone was going to see it. What if people didn't like that I was making money?

I blurted out the answer. In return, she shared her salary with me. As soon as I hung up, I called the Create & Cultivate editor into my office and told her what had transpired. "Do you think she's going to run that number?" I asked her. She kind of laughed and said, "Of course she's going to write about it. Your salary is now the most interesting part of the piece."

She was right. The piece came out. The title? "You'll Never Guess How Much This CEO Makes." Or something like that. But there was my nightmare. The number: $700K. Loud and proud for everyone to see! I was nervous for two reasons. First, it wasn't indicative of my standard yearly income by any means. I had sold my first company that year and had some luck in the stock market, and that number included those payouts, plus my salary at two (essentially) full-time jobs, plus my initial capital contribution back from C&C. Second, and this is very important, founders don't usually take a typical "salary." I wasn't getting a check twice a month to make sure my utilities stayed on! If the business made no money, I made no money. I paid myself and my partners through profit-sharing when we could, which is very standard for founders. Founders typically are the lowest-paid employees at most startups; they are focused on growing and building the team, not lining their pockets, and that is something I still practice.

Still, to my surprise, there was no backlash. No blacklisting. There was something really special about that moment—people were actually rooting for me. I never considered "money" a dirty word. I had learned along my career path thus far to ask for what I was worth. I had also been telling other women to do the same. But for some reason, until this point, the concepts of feminism and capitalism existed in two separate worlds—at least in my head.

Is it possible to be a feminist capitalist? I'd ask myself. Why do women seemed damned if they do make money and damned if they don't? These were fears I had. I don't know if you've noticed, but the court of public opinion is *flourishing* on social media. Keyboard warriors and trolls are quick to tell you what is wrong with your ideas, tactics, and shoe collection. Nothing is off-limits on the internet!

But in that moment when I spoke the number out loud, I assumed a power over my career that I had not yet experienced. I reconciled my feminist side with my capitalist side. Money was there to be made. It was there to be disseminated to *other* women. Yes, I do this because I believe in it, but I also do it because it's how I make my living. It is my *job*. I know some people would disagree with it, but I do think money is power.

And that's one of the best parts of being the boss. When you get to the place where you have decision-making power, you get to give that money to other people, and the majority of those people for me are women. Just like in *Spider-Man*, with great power comes great responsibility. Championing other female business owners. Becoming an angel investor in female-owned companies that deserve an angel. It also means promoting your current female employees and particularly placing women into positions of power.

So let's break down what that power and responsibility really look like in the workplace—and what you need to look out for, both as boss and employee.

First Things First: Interviewing and Hiring

Some of the best advice I've ever received is "Be slow to hire, quick to fire."

One of the most surreal parts of owning a business is when you realize you're ready to hire your first employee (or, if you're lucky, employees plural). When it comes to your employees, it's time to over-prepare.

That's right. It's not only the interviewee who should come ready to answer your questions. You need to have all the right questions in place. And, more importantly, realize that this is an interview to determine a mutually good fit. When I was starting out, I was trying too hard to sell people on the job and the company rather than determining if they were the right fit.

When it comes to interviewing, there needs to be honesty—on both sides.

Tips to Keep in Mind

+ Don't hire friends. Let's get this one out of the way immediately. It rarely, if ever, ends well.

+ Be careful not to make promises you can't keep about benefits, room for growth, or responsibilities. Of course things change along the way, but communication is key.

+ When posting your ad, use generic keywords that are easily searchable. You will find more applicants if you post "office manager" rather than something unique to your company like "director of happiness."

+ Clarify if the desired skills are mandatory, preferred, or a bonus. You don't want to waste time with applicants who don't meet your minimum qualifications, but you also don't want to miss out on good applicants just because they don't have some qualifications that aren't deal breakers for you.

+ Include a little about your company culture to attract people who will mix well with your personality and brand. It doesn't matter if they're a graphic design rock star or graduated from a top university—if they don't share your values, it's a no-go.

+ After the interview, check in with yourself and see if the candidate passes the "airport test." This is a super scientific methodology in which you honestly answer the question "If I were stranded in an airport for five hours with this person, would I be OK?" You want employees who you can tolerate for extended periods of time and who understand the need for strong carry-on luggage and in-flight Wi-Fi.

+ Ask what skills and experience your budget can afford—if you have a clear salary range and realistic expectations of what that person can and will do, you'll wind up with a better pool of applicants.

+ Do a three-month trial with everyone. Check in after three months and discuss how it's going, if it's a good fit, and where room for improvement lies.

+ Do a one-year review where employees evaluate themselves and get feedback from their peers (anonymously). This is a great way to pause and evaluate and hear from your employees in a nonscary format.

What to Look for to Build a Successful Small Team

Note that this is contingent on the type of boss you are. I am hyper-involved in the everyday but also require my team to take on a lot on their own. I have high expectations for work product and what my team is doing as it's all a representation of the company I have built—and that we are now building together. And lastly, communication is my love language. I love a good bullet-pointed list or a meeting recap. Pro tip: Find out your boss's love language immediately and react and adapt to it.

Key Team Vibes I Recommend to Any Business Owner

✦ Talent who can "wear many hats" and is down to jump in on things no matter whether the task falls under their job description or not.

✦ Someone who understands your company culture and mission and truly "gets it." I am always transparent about the long hours and how there is a lot of responsibility and self-motivation and self-management involved. Non-self-starters need not apply. Hence the next point . . .

✦ An independent self-starter who doesn't need hand-holding (that last bit I believe is crucial in today's work culture).

+ A team player everyone (whether that's just you or a small staff) will get along with.

+ An employee who is flexible and not set in their ways and is willing to learn from you.

+ Someone who has a sense of humor or at least a sense of reality and can handle feedback in constructive and lighthearted ways.

+ Someone who leads with positivity first. Negativity, client shit-talking, colleague shit-talking—it's all a slippery slope that works to bum everyone out. Yes, there will be hurdles, rude emails, and mistakes. This is pretty standard for human beings having a job. But I am not here for anyone's negativity impacting the group #vibe.

What I certainly look for, especially on a small team, is someone who loves hats. All of the hats. It's why you will still see me decaling at Create & Cultivate conferences. Egos have no place in a small biz, nor does being stuck in an old model or way of thinking. Dinosaurs are extinct for a reason. We are multihyphenate hustlers, and with the multilevel hustle, multiple talents are needed.

The ways in which people consume everything has changed significantly. So if we are not evolving, we are not doing our job. We want to help advance the new creators, the thinkers, the other dreamers. And we've only just begun. We don't want to create a pipeline of new workers; we want to burst open the whole channel and see what happens. (This *is* a WorkParty after all.)

How do you find those people? Ask a lot of questions. Ask all of the questions.

Three questions that I ALWAYS ask in interviews are:

✦ "Tell me about something in the industry we work in that you thought worked well, and something you didn't." This is about paying attention to the industry you are in—if they can't mention anything, they aren't paying attention.

✦ "Please provide a case study detailing a project you're proud of or that performed well." Numbers are key—for instance, "I grew X community by 75 percent in three months by implementing Y."

✦ "What are your views on work-life balance? Are you down to give up time and energy for a company you believe in?" People often instinctively will answer yes to this, but press them on this, it's important.

The question about work-life balance will always give me insight into what kind of worker someone is. And there is no wrong answer here. The goal is to find the people who will work in your environment, and if weekends are required, it's important to note that. You're essentially going on a first date and asking someone to marry you. It's a big commitment, so don't take it lightly.

Some other specific questions to ask that will tell you more about someone's character, not their KPIs (key performance indicators).

✦ "Tell me about a time when you took on responsibilities outside your job description or department."

✦ "When you want to tackle a project outside of your usual role, how do you communicate this with teammates and your manager?"

✦ "If you realize that you can't complete an assignment by the deadline, how do you communicate that?"

✦ "What are some things that influence your personal brand?"

By taking what may feel like *tedious* time in the hiring process, you will save yourself time and money in the long run. People are a company's best assets, so take your time in developing them, and once you find the "one," help them grow.

Studies on the cost of employee turnover are all over the board. Some studies (such as one from the Society for Human Resource Management) predict that every time a business replaces a salaried employee, it costs six to nine months' salary on average. For a manager making $40,000 a year, that's $20,000 to $30,000 in recruiting and training expenses.

Which brings us to my next point: Your small business will feel like your extended family. You know, those people you love but who drive you insane?

You spend more time with them than you do with your spouse, boyfriend, friends, and family combined (#sorrymom). There are shared lunches and late hours, and at certain points, you all wear every single hat. Because when you're working to build something together, you switch hats, pants, shoes; the words "I can't do that" or "That's not my job" are not part of your vocabulary. In many ways, each of you is the "ideal worker"—something that gender and labor scholars have identified as the person who shows up early, leaves late, never says no, never gets sick, answers emails morning, noon, night, weekends, makes every meeting, is a go-getter, ad infinitum. These are employees who work hard and challenge themselves on a daily basis. In a dream world, every team member of your startup is that person.

Here on earth, however, there are specific people who fit better into certain roles and make the squad function like a well-oiled machine. So these are the six employees I think every single startup needs.

1. The Visionary

The Visionary is often the CEO. They think big and small; they see far ahead but also catch the tiniest of details right in the moment, the little things you would never even notice. Nothing gets past them, but it's because the Visionary knows how they want to see their vision executed. Thinking outside the box is one part of their supernatural abilities. They are highly functional, fast-paced, and fastidious. You often hear their footsteps from down the hall before you see them in the flesh.

2. The Closer

The Closer has perseverance and structure like you wouldn't believe and a solution to any problem. In part, it's because she's "been there, done that," and brings experience from many industries to the table. She knows how to work a conversation to her advantage. She is great at team management and turning ideas into action items—especially at executing the vision of the dreamer. She doesn't take things personally and knows the difference between "ass" and "assertive."

3. The Unicorn

Part social butterfly, part go-getter, the Unicorn of the bunch is known for making magic and doing it with pep and a smile. From meeting with clients to working with talent, she's the ultimate team player because part of that sociable charm is inherent to a caregiver—keeping team morale up even as stress rises. It's not magic; it's about chemistry, about making a room feel at ease by making every person feel taken care of. The Unicorn will treat everyone as an individual so your company will stand out as a whole. The Unicorn keeps the momentum going.

4. The No-Nonsense Type

Follow-through is one of the main traits of the no-nonsense employee. Enthusiastic but firm, the No-Nonsense Type is a bit like sandpaper—

firm, tough, but able to smooth out anything. You need a nose-to-the-grindstone, no-nonsense worker who will always be crystal clear on what she needs—especially if she doesn't like the way you're doing something. She is firm, tenacious, and knows to get everything in writing. The No-Nonsense Type knows that if you miss one detail, Rome topples. And we've already learned that lesson. From big picture to the nitty-gritty, nothing is falling apart on the no-nonsense watch, even if it means a sternly worded convo or two.

5. The Heart

You know the person. She's always saying yes. She is there to talk out an idea
with you, jump in, give you her thoughts,
and share her best ideas—all the while
grinding out what's on her own plate.
The Heart is less concerned with
credit than with crafting the right message. The Heart knows it's important
that everyone on the team be on message as
well. Which, yes, means breaking from a to-do list and jumping in
where the Heart is needed.

6. The Pistol

A bit of a self-motivated worker bee, the Pistol is a straight shooter
who fires off ideas and gets work done at the same speed. The Pistol

doesn't wait for ideas to come to her, nor
does she second-guess herself. The Pistol
is always innovating. Always providing the
best. That means tons of ideas. Plenty
of which get thrown out. But the Pistol
will keep shooting and shooting straight.
Sometimes this means asking for forgive-
ness instead of permission.

So that's the dream. But what happens when the dream doesn't
come to life in quite the way you imagined?

Oof, We Gotta Talk about Firing

I told you the best advice I ever received was to be slow to hire, quick to fire. It sounds a little callous, but hear me out.

Cutting the cord with an employee is never pleasant. Even if it's 100 percent the right thing to do. Even if they are the worst employee on earth. And that is an incredibly hard lesson to learn—especially when you have to let go of a day-one. It happens, and it's one of the hardest experiences to have, but keeping an employee who doesn't fit will make more work for you. And it will make everyone miserable, including the employee.

The thing about firing people is oftentimes, unbeknownst to the person being fired, it's mutual. They might not know it, but if things are not working out, it's important to realize it's not working on their end either.

So there can be a humanity to firing someone, but there are legal parameters to think about as well. There needs to be "cause" to fire people. So first things first, have the tough conversation about it not being a fit, and oftentimes, if they agree, it's a simple mutual split. If not, it's a bit more difficult; you have to make a case for the firing. So it's important to document the wrongdoings moving forward. This is why the three-month trial period is key—it's a moment of reflection, a time to let people know it's not working without the heart-wrenching process of firing.

My advice? You gotta rip the Band-Aid off, before the one bad egg employee rips your company apart. Once you've built your stellar squad, it doesn't necessarily get easier. If I'm being honest, some days it feels like the more people I hire, the harder I work. In part, that's because letting go is one of the hardest things to do.

Reasons for firing an employee vary. Sometimes they simply aren't performing well. Other times they consistently show up late and are unreliable. Team vibes matter. If there is a member of your team who is constantly letting the crew down, you need to let them go. You can't sacrifice an entire team because you don't want to have an uncomfortable conversation with one person. Practically speaking, the easiest way to fire someone is end of day on a Friday. It's way less dramatic and traumatic (for everyone) than making them pack up their desk Monday morning.

And there will be drama.

Because when you've built something from the ground up, it's your kid. No other way around it. And sending that kid off to school to have other teachers mold its mind (or in this case its brand and how it presents itself to the world) can be torture.

But if you want to grow, you have to be able to let go. Everyone does this in their own time and in their own way. Being a boss has its ups and downs, no doubt about that, but if you only take away one thing from this chapter, it's this: Never doubt yourself. You've got to be your own business BFF.

chapter eight

On Boys and Business and the Illusory "Work-Life Balance"

There's a saying in production: It can be fast, cheap, or beautiful, but it can only be two out of the three.

Put another way: You can't have it all. Often preached at women who want to have careers, families, and, you know, independent lives.

Our dear Sarah Jessica Parker, my beloved Carrie Bradshaw,* even played a protagonist in what should be a contender for most tone-deaf movie title of 2011: *I Don't Know How She Does It*. The movie's about a woman trying to build a successful career, have a family, and be a loving wife. Spoiler alert: She's barely getting by, and she spends eighty-nine minutes incredibly stressed the fuck out trying to "do it all!"

This narrative is all too common for women. Somehow an un-

---

*I know. I know. I know. Even though we all wanted to be Carrie, we really should have all wanted to be Miranda. Rewatch *SATC* as a feminist adult and you'll likely take serious issue with Carrie's life choices. Miranda I can get behind. (You just need to be intentional with your time and emotions. And stop spending all your energy chasing Mr. Big and start chasing Mr. My Big Dreams.)

derlying assumption seems to be that it is magically easier for men to be good husbands, fathers, and CEOs. But women are the ones who are stressed out about it. The common hum of women everywhere saying, "I just want a solid marriage, good friendships, and a successful business" is often met with, "You can only have two of the three."

To channel Carrie Bradshaw, I couldn't help but wonder: Is there truth to this rule of two-thirds? Can you only have 66.66666666666666 percent of your dreams at any given time?

I'm here to assert, with a genuine note of optimism, that it's doable, though the road to doable is a rough one. But the good news is you *can* have it all.

In the spirit of honesty, vulnerability, and reflection, I will share with you three personal truths:

1. I have been in three major relationships in my adult years. I have two ex-boyfriends in Los Angeles, and I am married to my third boyfriend, David. I do not speak to my exes, but was just informed one of them moved a few blocks down from me because the universe has a weird sense of humor. The second ex is a charming sociopath whom I hope never to see again.

2. I spent the formative, early years of Create & Cultivate single as fuck and third-wheeling. As bummed out as I could get during those years, I'm really happy it went down that way.

3. I met my husband on Tinder, and despite joking about it, I would never say we met at Trader Joe's. I'm not ashamed that an app brought us together!

I can only reflect on my (admittedly heteronormative) relationships as, well, a straight woman. Which is to say: I will share with you my experiences, and I hope that the takeaways can be universal.

My first relationship was with, drumroll please, a coworker! I don't believe in hard-and-fast rules, but, ladies, be very careful with this one. There will likely be a time when a coworker behaves like . . . not a coworker. Making friends and meeting lovers is a challenge post college, and in life in general as a busy human, and as a result, one makes business BFFs (roll call, chapter 6!) in the workplace, and sometimes, when teams and meetings and late work hours cosmically align, coworkers can become coworkers with benefits.

If the stars really align, a coworker-with-benefits situation can become a secret relationship in the workplace. If you crank the relationship dial one more notch, you can file the paperwork and become HR-official, corporate America's version of a promise ring. Or at least, this was the case with my first official adult boyfriend in Los Angeles, who we will refer to as the Corporate Climber.

The Corporate Climber was charming at first. He seemed to not only accept my ambition but encourage it. (The operative word there is "seemed.")

We were the heads of our respective departments. I felt powerful. I was in a new city, with new friends and a new man? This seemed to be going too well. I began dating the Corporate Climber shortly after my cross-country move, which made easing into a new city . . . well, easier. I was twenty-three, felt like I was starting to become a thought leader in my career, and had found a partner who was on a similar trajectory.

We were a power couple in the way that mid-twenty-somethings can be. I liked the way we looked, and people liked the way we looked together. On paper, we were perfect. He was an alpha male, and I

often followed his lead. In new territory for me, I was very much playing the role of the girl-next-door girlfriend I hadn't before.

The last guy I had dated before the Corporate Climber was a vol-
atile club promoter in New York, and I was eager to prove that I was
"relationship material," whatever that means. Only now that I look
back on it do I realize that I was playing a role and walking on egg-
shells, shedding the most important parts of my personality along
the way.

That became apparent one morning in the car on the way to work.
We were carpooling, a relationship perk in the land of lonely commut-
ing, and he was preparing for his one-year review at the company. I
gave him a pep talk and encouraged him when he said he wanted to
ask for a higher salary.

"I want to be making at least six figures," I remember him griping.

I nearly choked and was able to get out, "Yeah! You definitely
should be!"

He paused. Did he notice the inflection in my voice—the pause
or maybe the choke? A few minutes went by and he asked, "Wait . . .
What do you make?"

My stomach churned. I felt the power dynamic shift. I was making more money than him. And he had just caught on to that.

I tried to back-pedal. I told him I had just been given a bump to
$105,000 (not true).* It wasn't a big deal (not true). I tried to deflect.
I told him it was because I lived in NYC and salaries were different
there (somewhat true), but the worst part was, I didn't just own it. I

---

*This is a lot of money. I don't want to downplay it or let you think that I am throwing six-figure
salaries around unappreciatively. Salaries are not always linear or on upward trajectories. I was
not yet twenty-five and making over $100,000, mostly because I was on the forefront of an
emerging market that brands and businesses were starting to seriously invest in. It was equal
parts skill, determination, and market opportunity (and yes, my working-class parents did ask
me if I was dealing drugs). I've taken pay cuts since this time. I've made more since then, too.
I know it's an uncomfy topic. But I don't want it to be, and we'll talk more about money in the
next chapter.

deserved that salary. I worked my ass off for that salary. That moment was a true low point, downplaying what I had earned to make a man feel better about himself. And yes, this makes sense in certain situations, but not in love and partnership and transparency, all of which are part of a healthy relationship dynamic.

Things changed after that. His rooting for my success turned more into resentment. Work became a taboo topic, and since we were coworkers, it was, of course, complicated and, slowly things got worse.

He dumped me two months later. He just looked at me and told me he never loved me and so on, so forth. The breakup was brutal but probably exactly what the doctor ordered for his broken ego. He made me feel small, not special, and not important. He seemed to want me to be disposable because I had power over him. The setting of this chat, BTW: my Prius. The same location where he had learned I was earning more money than him. It was a smart car all right. One that knew exactly what I needed.

Months later, I found out a few things from someone at work that threw salt in my healing wounds.

When I revealed over coffee that I had been dating the Corporate Climber, our former colleague scrunched his face. "I just feel so bad telling you this," he told me. "I sat in on a meeting where he blatantly said you should be let go. He said you were the last to be hired, so should be first to be fired." This is NOT, I'd like to note, anything like "slow to hire, quick to fire." His logic, which my bosses had clearly listened to, is not good biz advice.

I felt like I was going to throw up. I couldn't believe it would come down to that, but it all clicked into place. The picture became clear—who he was and who I became around him became crystal clear. Shortly after I had revealed my higher salary, my alpha male partner could not cope with this information. He was in a meeting, one where

I was *conveniently* left off the calendar invite, and advocated for my position to be terminated. And the rest, as they say, was history.

The Corporate Climber's true colors had come out. He liked that I was successful, but his ego didn't want me to be *too* successful and, god forbid, more successful than him. Who I was and, more importantly, who I was trying to be shattered the narrative his ego had assigned to me. Good-on-paper doesn't always translate to happily-ever-after.

Some men, especially men in the workplace, cannot separate their egos from who they are and what they say they believe. For a year, the Corporate Climber was my number-one cheerleader, told me he loved me, and lobbied for me to make waves in my career and the company we worked for. But once our relationship reached critical mass, and once I broke the script he had assumed for me, he lobbied for me to leave. Leave our workplace and our relationship.

I learned one major professional and personal lesson after the Corporate Climber exited stage left: Power structures exist in every relationship. As far as personal relationships were concerned, I now knew I needed a partner secure in his skin. Someone who wouldn't be insecure about a salary discrepancy and someone whose ego I didn't feel I needed to tiptoe around. And I will admit, that was a hard nut to crack.

By now you know about the meltdowns and pizza and subsequent business building that happened after the Corporate Climber and I broke up. You also know I found my person later on, so this is not meant to be a total bummer. It's a cautionary tale for those workplace relationships that may present themselves. Work can often be isolating and intimate, and as we've established, there's solace in the shared experience. It's too easy when you're in the trenches with people to forget about boundaries, to want to be even closer to the people who share your experiences for forty to fifty hours a week. Especially when your coworker is attractive, and there's chemistry, and the only other promising relationship in your life is with your Netflix account (#sponsoredbyNetflix #justkiddingbutshouldbe).

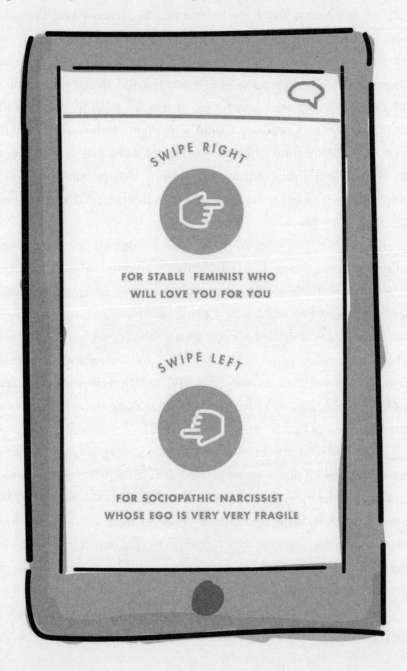

But remember that for every exception to the rule, and for every wedding you attend in your late twenties for people who met at work and think it was serendipity, there is another failed workplace relationship to counter it. Remember earlier when I said I've never been confused for a hopeless romantic? I know this sounds cynical, but I'm a realist. As we rise together, ladies, we're going to challenge the patriarchy's egos. And if you're used to the pendulum of privilege swinging your way for all of history, equality can feel like an injustice. The Corporate Climber was not a feminist (despite the fact he probably thinks he is) and did not want to see me succeed on my terms. I'm grateful for the lessons that relationship taught me. And I'm grateful to have a sense of self stronger than any heartbreak.

It took me two years to bounce back from my great Corporate Climber backstabbing. But time heals all wounds, ladies. I remained single through the early days of my first business, going on dates every few months just to make sure I could still have a conversation with the opposite sex. I asked to be set up with my friends' eligible friends, which takes a certain level of humility and vulnerability. Nothing panned out, and most second dates were indefinitely postponed, ending with a text sent by either one of us, claiming to be "sooooo busy the next few weeks, but let's catch up soon."

Enter my second official adult boyfriend, who we will refer to as the Rom-Com Villain. We met at a music festival, which is pretty high up there on the meet-cute trope list. Furthermore, the Rom-Com Villain is the boyfriend the protagonist believes to be her one true love, but the audience can tell he's a fake from day one. The protagonist has tunnel vision and is blind to his flaws, while the audience cringes at what a try-hard he is.

He was a talent manager for one of the biggest talent agencies in Hollywood. I'd liken him to Ben Stiller's character in *Reality Bites*, except I'm not Winona Ryder and I don't have a brooding Ethan Hawke in my life. My Rom-Com Villain was charming, energetic, funny, and the king of small talk. He used product in his hair and drove a new BMW and was always on the guest list somewhere. He grew up well-to-do in Los Angeles and had private school pals, celebrity friends, and a laundry list of connections. I was hungry to meet more entre-preneurs and industry veterans in Los Angeles, and he seemed like the perfect man to tackle life with, plus he gave me access to the shiny glitz of a scene I wasn't privy to (ahem, Hollywood), which seemed like a nice alternative to my startup world.

There's only so much I want to put in writing about the end of my relationship with the Rom-Com Villain, but it wasn't pretty. I want to note, this paralleled the time with business-partner breakup, so I was in a particularly vulnerable place. And over time, I saw a different side of him. A controlling side. An emotionally abusive side. A scary side. The man I had fallen in love with, who he had represented himself to be, was not who he truly was, and therein lies the villain trope: The protagonist is never supposed to end up with the two-faced, sleazy Hollywood manager. She's not supposed to end up with the partner who doesn't support her new business, who gets mad at her for devot-ing time to her business or friends, who rages with jealousy, or who doubts her capabilities. She's not supposed to settle for half-baked support and emotional gaslighting.

The truth is, I still carry some guilt over how long I stayed with my Rom-Com Villain. He fractured many of my relationships, creating a divide between me and my friends. He told me about a "crazy ex-girlfriend" and what a psycho, vindictive, petty "bitch" she was.* I gull-ibly ate up every word, only to be told later that not only were he and

---

*Red flag! Red flag! Always look at the narrative your partner creates around their past rela-tionships. Is there respect there? Did they learn anything? Are they harboring unaddressed or suppressed feelings toward their ex? Any use of the word "bitch" is a no-no.

his ex still friends who hung out and spoke regularly, but he had fueled the fire between the women in his life: he was bad-mouthing me to his mother, his sister, his ex-girlfriend-but-still-friend, and other female peers. In hindsight, I now understand why I always felt lonely and unwelcome with our peers when we were out—it was because he didn't want me getting too close to the other women in his life. He didn't want me to find out that he was still canoodling with his ex or casting doubt on my business (and mental health) to his well-connected-in-the-industry mom and sister. And I doubted myself and leaned into the codependency of our relationship. It wasn't healthy.

And then one day, your older sister no longer recognizes the voice on the other side of the iPhone. My sister flew to California to take me on a seven-day escape from reality, an intervention to get me back to my normal self, to get me over a toxic relationship. We drove north up Highway 1, stopping in Santa Barbara and Big Sur and all the dramatic cliffs on the California coast as I cried and cried and, yes, cried some more.

The closest person to me in my life no longer recognized me, which is important. Why? Because we can—and have to—do this for other women, lift them up, pull them back to themselves. Emotional and sometimes physical abuse can happen to even the strongest of women, and it can be recognized and intervened upon. I couldn't pull myself out of the situation I was in, despite the fact that everyone was telling me to leave. Sometimes you need to be physically plucked out of your surroundings.

Life is not a movie, guys. So this protagonist spent some years on her own and marinated on what matters most. If you picked up on the foreshadowing, this is the part where I stay single. AF. I was building a business, and everything inside of me said that was my priority, not courtship.

I also think that loneliness is a spectrum, and certain points of that spectrum are different shades of pain. There's the fresh pain that comes after a breakup when your bed feels like the loneliest place on earth. There's the loneliness that comes from going to a wedding alone, and attempting to answer the most iconic, perplexing question all single people will be asked in their lifetimes: "So, how are you still single?" Actress, life coach, and please-be-my-BFF Tracee Ellis Ross told the room at the 2017 *Glamour* Women of the Year Awards: "I also dreamed of winning an Oscar and being on the cover of magazines and making a difference in the world, helping women find our voices. And from that dreaming, I have built an incredible life. I have become a woman that I am proud to be.

"And then someone tells me about their friend who adopted a child at fifty-two and how 'it's never too late for your life to have meaning,' and my worth gets diminished as I am reminded that I have 'failed' on the marriage and carriage counts. Me! This bold, liberated, independent woman. I mean, I work out, eat well, I mostly show up to work on time, I'm a good friend, a solid daughter, a hard worker, my credit is good, I take out the garbage before it gets smelly, I recycle, and I won a Golden Globe! I'm killing it! So, why? Why do I get snagged this way? As if all that I have done and who I am doesn't matter."

And it's so true. Women get snagged and snag themselves this way. "How are you still single?" is a question I never want to hear asked of another woman ever again. We are not defined by our relationship status. We define ourselves. Alone doesn't mean lonely.

More so, there's a kind of loneliness that doesn't feel particularly painful. The sort of loneliness in which you accept that you're going to be alone for a while, that you're mentally taking yourself out of the running for a romantic lead. It's not giving up, per se; it's just putting romantic priorities on pause. Again, Carrie never really got this. Miranda was ready to raise a kid on her own and keep her job.

This is where the hopeful romantics will tell you (and tell you and tell you) that "you find love when you least expect it!" I believe that to be mostly true, but I think it's possible to avoid finding love altogether if you're hell-bent on prioritizing other stuff, e.g., a business and mental clarity.

So I avoided finding love during the formative years of Create & Cultivate. This is not to say I had a line of bachelors out my door, begging for my affections. I simply invested all of my free time into my business, my new role as a solo CEO, and my female friendships. I spent a summer in Portland subletting an apartment in a basement just because I needed to get out of Dodge. I reinvested in my relationships with my ride-or-dies. I started new rituals. I got my aforementioned "therapy dog" terrier Noah, who, according to paperwork, is an anxiety dog, despite the fact that he's more anxious than I am. I moved back to Los Angeles after my hiatus in Portland and moved into a house. When the unit in back of my home opened up, my ride-or-die Rachel moved in.

Enter David, stage right. Two years into Create & Cultivate, I was going through an online dating binge, and by "binge," I mean swiping right and never actually meeting anyone. I think I was trying to prove that I could finally open myself up to dating now that my business was a toddler and learning how to walk on its own. I went on a select few dates with guys who were . . . How do I say this? *The worst.* Some were freaked out by my ambition. When they saw the house I lived in alone, or when I told them about C&C's momentum, they recoiled. The cycle was almost like a game to watch.

Then something unexpected happened. I went on a first date that didn't suck.

David was a soft-spoken art director for a big branding agency, lived in Venice, and had a penchant for graffiti. He had crooked teeth and sleeve tattoos and an irresistible laugh. So I did what any rational woman who hadn't felt seen, really *seen*, by a man for years would do: I drank. Heavily. We met at a bar by my house in the Los Feliz neighborhood. We didn't stop talking. I invited him back to my house for another drink. Realizing that my level of drunkenness and my forward invitation might not be giving off the message that I was trying to send (that I was emotionally stable and ready for a partner in crime!), again I did what a rational woman would do: I force-invited my friends Dana and Delia over. They were in the neighborhood, and I lured them to my house with the promise of more wine and single men. (There were no single men aside from David.)

True to form, my girlfriends came over to investigate this offering of wine and single men. They quickly realized there was only wine, their friend on a first date, and her dog having a meltdown over the entire thing. They humored me by drinking with David and me in my front yard, essentially joining in on our first date. I had been seeing (and paying for) a numerologist at that time, and in an effort to impress my impromptu party guests, I told everyone what their birthdays could predict about their personalities.

I'm pretty sure none of it was accurate. My loving friends assured me the next day that he was great but I had been drunk and kind of mean and likely wouldn't be getting a call back from David.

But, much to their surprise, they were wrong! Turns out, when you meet your person, they don't care so much how many glasses of rosé you drink, or if you invite your friends to crash the first date, or if you don't actually know how to talk about the niche study of numerology. Turns out, when someone sees you for you, they appreciate the parts of your personality you always thought were a turnoff. He liked me for my ambitious, talkative self. He liked that I worked late and went to networking events and traveled a lot. Turns out, your person comes around when you get out of the rom-com in your head and stop trying to write the role for who you think fits in your fantasy narrative.

You know how this ends up, so I'll spare you the mushy-gushy love story that followed. I truly feel in my core that I met David when I stopped trying to be someone I wasn't in relationships. I was over trying to play the "cool girl," mostly because it was tiring to pretend that I wasn't a hungry entrepreneur or hungry human who put work over boys and actually wanted the burger over the salad.

Having a true sense of self and knowing how a partner can add value to your already-enough self can be powerful. And I refuse to buy into the shame that some people associate with online dating. I may have been introduced to David by an app, but I *met* him in a bar in Los Feliz on a Saturday night in February. I was building a business and busy and trying to be intentional with my time. I wasn't interested in going to a bar, sipping a martini by myself, like characters do in sitcoms. I wasn't going to devote endless hours to searching for my Mr. Big, but swiping on an app was doable within my schedule.

I'm a firm believer that you get from online dating what you put into it. I was twenty-nine, done fucking around, and felt more like myself than ever. I had been through hell and back with my last relationship, and I knew what I wanted and what I was willing to put up with. I didn't need a joker or a corporate climber with a five-year plan—I needed someone who wanted to love me, be my ally, and encourage me to flourish.

If you're in a single zone right now, think really hard about what you truly need—as opposed to want—in a partner. All the same guys are on the same apps, but with a little bit of scrutiny, honesty, and good intentions, you can be introduced to someone special. And if you take the leap, you can choose to still have that meet-cute in a bar, on your terms, of course. Just like the rest of your life.

And, oh yeah, career.

Let's get back to that.

chapter nine

The Negotiations

Your entire career is a negotiation. *Ooh, this chapter sounds like fun!*

I'll tell you what. Make it through this chapter and I'll [insert something you want here]. Shake on it? Good. Let's continue. That's negotiation!

Every day you are making decisions that affect you, your employees, your family. Whether these are small negotiations you make with yourself (e.g., going with your gut versus going with the numbers) or larger negotiations you're making in a room filled with people (e.g., is it time to sell?!), they are happening on the micro and macro levels day in and day out.

As a female founder, I've experienced the dramatic swing of the gender-imbalance issue. At the start of my first company, I noticed that my fees nearly always came up for negotiation—seemingly just because I was a female business owner sitting across the table from clients. In the beginning, to test the theory, I brought male employees with me into key meetings regarding fees to gauge the difference. Across the board, the fee bargaining didn't occur when they were present, and most of the tough questions were directed to my male intern. My *intern*!

But this presented a catch-22 for me, one that other entrepreneurs have probably faced, too. I wanted (and needed) to take on the new business and grow my portfolio, but that meant sometimes giving in to lower, negotiated fees—essentially saying yes to gendered pay inequality.

Now, at Create & Cultivate, we work with Fortune 500 clients, and we can turn down business when the numbers don't add up. I think the elusive "boys' club" that revolves mostly around startup funding, handshake deals, and venture capital will always be present in some iteration. However, I've seen the clouds parting, with more women at the helm of large budgets and leading prominent companies. That's why it's important for more women to excel in the financial aspects of running a business and managing the budgets, especially when it comes to funding, investing, and raising money so we can help balance gender inequality and get more money in the hands of women entrepreneurs.

Getting comfortable with negotiation is part of the ride. So let's break down the most common types of negotiations you're already having (without even realizing it!).

The "How Much Do I Show?" Instagram Negotiation

This may seem like a softball negotiation, but your personal online brand will be a part of your success or failure, whether you like it or not. We've all seen the Insta-perfect life. And we've seen bloggers and influencers build million-dollar businesses off of Instagram.

For a lot of us, Instagram can be our weapon of choice when it comes to dominating the social media game. Unlike Twitter and Facebook, it is one of the social media channels where you can express yourself or your brand creatively and really put your best foot forward when it comes to building a great visual aesthetic.

For a while, it was all about getting your grid right. However, with the introduction of Instagram Stories, it was clear that people wanted to see behind the scenes, the everyday, minute by minute. They wanted to get to know the people behind the filters.

I've done it. I'm still on my grid grind, and more often than not I advise other female entrepreneurs to think *brand first*. However, I have to acknowledge that more and more people are letting their audience know the real them, not just the #goals version. And audiences are responding in droves.

Inspirational speaker and stylist Ruthie Lindsey had a rather large following on Instagram. There were beautiful Nashville dinners. Inspirational frolicking shots of a beautiful, long-legged Lindsey in harvest fields. Her life looked, by any account, perfect. Insta-perfect.

Behind the scenes was a much different story. In truth, Ruthie spent the majority of her twenties confined to her bed. There was an accident her senior year of high school, then recovery. Then, years later, came an intense pain that "shot up her head." Multiple doctors had no answers. Scans were read wrong for years, until finally one doctor figured out that a wire from a spinal cord surgery had pierced into her brain stem. Shocked that she wasn't paralyzed, they operated and removed the piece. A new pain ensued. Nothing helped. And the pain-medication dependence dominoed.

But all dominoes can be reset. Picked up. And Ruthie realized she didn't want to live confined to pain; sunlight would be the best antidote. Her life started to change, and so did her Instagram account, now filled with honest anecdotes and the truth and a viral video she shared with her followers in which Ruthie says of the pain, "I would pinch myself to draw blood because I thought I was living in a nightmare." Direct messages rolled in from hundreds of strangers on social media, and people responded. They responded to her story. To her truth. And, yes, to the pain.

Now, you might be thinking, *I don't have a story like that* or *I'm not comfortable letting people in.* However, being yourself will help you avoid the addiction of "like" chasing. You know, only posting things that you think your audience wants to see. People pleasing won't get you anywhere, and after a while people will start to see through it. You don't have to give your innermost self, but you do need to embrace all of your facets, not just the pretty ones.

Now, yes. I called this a softball negotiation. But in some ways, it's not. If you choose to have a public Instagram, that "brand" is the face that you're putting out into the business world. You don't have to self-censor, but a general rule of thumb is to be intentional and honest with yourself about what you value. If you want to work with corporate America, you can't complain about your clients on Instagram Stories while driving home from a meeting.

The same goes for the political. And to be a woman right now is to be political.

If you decided to post #metoo like masses of other women or you decided to post your photos from the Women's March in January of 2017 and you lost followers, it really is NBD. What IS a huge deal is silencing your voice for the promise (or hope) of a like. It's not worth it.

Silence is actually not golden in the digital age; it's deafening.

Everyone has their social boundaries, and in order to succeed, you need to figure out what yours are. Maybe you have many. Maybe you have none. Whatever way your Instagram cookie crumbles is fine by me.

The "How Mad Should I Be?" Copycat Negotiation

When you create something from your soul, build something special, copycats will follow. It's the flip side of the success coin.

And that's not a bad thing. You just have to be prepared.

The whitespace is an exciting place to tap into. Opportunity abounds, and you're making the rules up as you go. But you need to know that once the dollars start flowing, other people will follow suit and use your experience as a case study to build a competitive business. Again, don't hate the player, hate the game.

We're in an era of on-demand services, and our smartphones have helped pave the way for a new marketplace of brands and services for consumers who need anything. Literally anything. This phenomenon has created a stark white canvas for new businesses to disrupt and shape the consumer landscape and its respective demands. We can all point to Silicon Valley's top-tier examples. Uber tapped into the whitespace of ride-sharing, which not only disrupted the taxi industry but also created a competitive landscape for brands like Lyft, Via, and Gett. Blue Apron initially made waves in the subscription-service sector by delivering consumers original recipes and perfectly portioned ingredients, which then gave way to HelloFresh, Purple Carrot, Green Chef, and a whole bunch more. Airbnb found the whitespace in travel and accommodations and dominated the likes of VRBO and Home-Away. These companies are your Silicon Valley tech darlings, all voted "Most Likely to Succeed" in their suburban high schools. If these companies were people, they would have perfect hair, clear skin, and a killer zip code.

While this on-demand era is efficient and convenient (wine delivery? I'm here for that), it's also taught a lot of us young entrepreneurs firsthand about competition and how success breeds it. I consider myself one of those #blessed entrepreneurs who have learned about copycats firsthand.

I launched Create & Cultivate in 2011, and four years of hard work and collaboration and decision making taught me how special the opportunity was. I saw the power in a platform, and the power of putting together something by millennial women for millennial women.

It took another three years of work after the ah-ha moment to develop the incredible platform we have today. None of this happened overnight, and I had to do a lot of exploratory and experimental work to find my audience. But that hadn't stopped the copycats from doing their thing. Every single day, I seem to stumble upon a new "workshop for entrepreneurial women looking to cultivate creativity." Once I found a site that was using images from our conference to promote their newly launched conference. One time, I caught wind that a competitor was using the exact same copy that we had used in a Create & Cultivate sales deck to sell sponsorships for their own female-driven conference. Major publications have plagiarized content from our blog.

Sometimes I feel like waving a white flag—hey, can't we all just get along? Sometimes I feel like throwing a red one—freakin' penalty time. Most days I do neither, but keep truckin' along like I always have.

So many innovators have felt the same pain. Jihan Zencirli, founder and head creative of Geronimo Balloons, told us that she's tagged *every. single. day.* in work that's not hers. "To be frank, I'm annoyed. It bums me out that what I do is now so common," she says. "When people copy me, I think, 'You saw this trend and you want a piece of that and you think it's beautiful. I can accept that for you. That's the way *you're* going to move forward and create a balloon business.'" But that's not what it started as for her.

She says she get emails all the time from people asking how to create a balloon business. Her response is simple: "You just find out," she says. "There's no one way to do anything. It's not my job to teach someone something that should be coming from their heart. Copying another company and their desires and their goals and their living is never going to reach people. To the untrained eye, they may look better. It may be a better product. But I like living in a world where people know there is a human being connected to it. Someone who is trying to create a thing of beauty and not just create a trend."

In the digital age of #bitchstolemylook, where so many things feel like *Blade Runner* replicants, this is incredibly pertinent and poignant advice. No one can copy your heart. Not even the folks in Silicon Valley 3D-printing organs. I've carried this through every year at Create & Cultivate. Even when other female-centric conferences pop up (and they do, a lot!), I remind myself that no one can copy my heart, or my hustle, and I'm good. (Most days.)

Sure, people will use your experiences as a case study to build a competitive business. It can feel personally and professionally crushing. If what you're doing is innovative and forward-thinking, if you are first to market, you will breed copycats. After (admittedly) spending too much time focusing on the competitors around me, I developed a mental exercise to not let myself get down on my own journey. This is where I fully recommend treating copycats like an ex-partner and making this your manifesto:

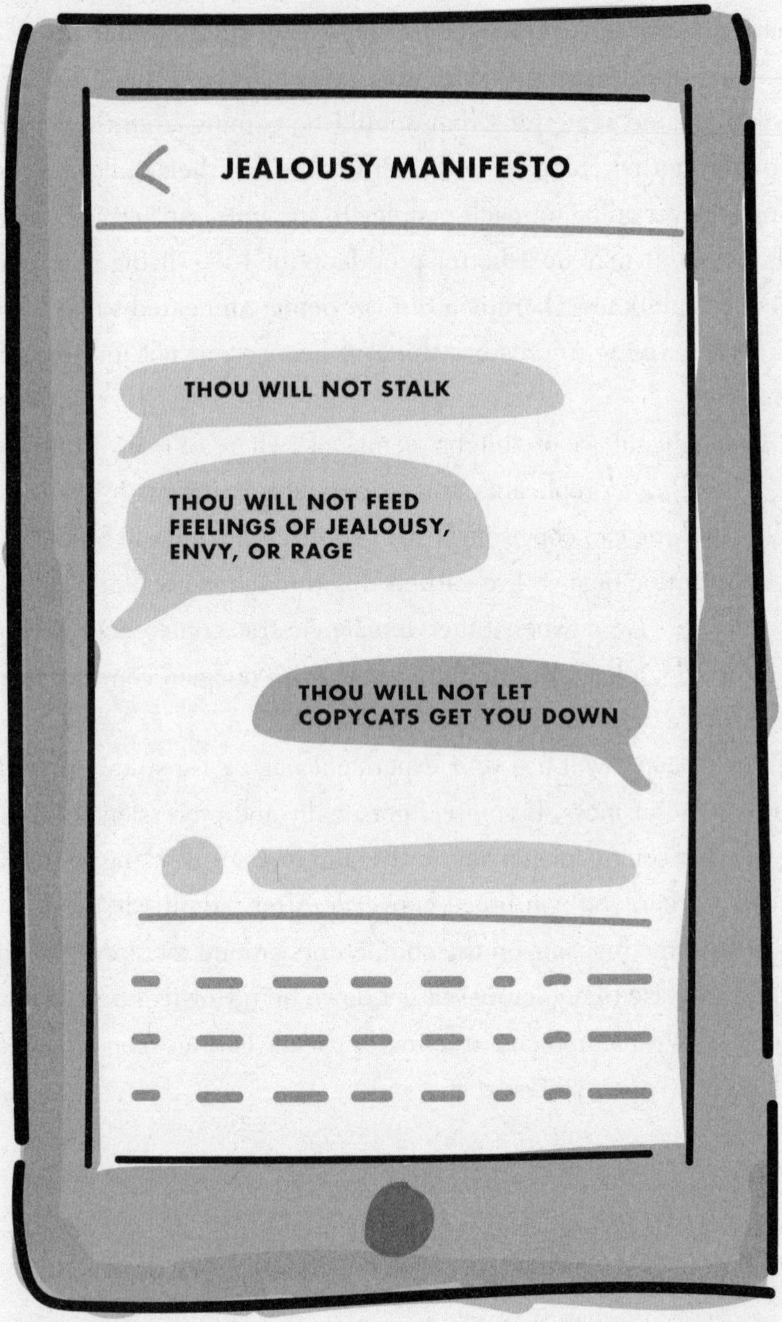
JEALOUSY MANIFESTO
THOU WILL NOT STALK
THOU WILL NOT FEED FEELINGS OF JEALOUSY, ENVY, OR RAGE
THOU WILL NOT LET COPYCATS GET YOU DOWN

It's too easy to fall down the competition rabbit hole, checking Instagram handles and reading into subtweets on your way down. But that energy has a better purpose, which is to fuel you, your ideas, and your vision. Think of your brain as emotional real estate. You don't want to give your competition too much free real estate in your head, or they'll take away from your creative real estate, your passionate real estate, and your entrepreneurial real estate.

Be a good property manager! Your brain and those who love you will thank you.

The "Do I Smile and Laugh This Off?" Negotiation

Back in Y2K someone let all the dogs out, and perhaps unfortunately, we still don't know why. But in 2017, there was a reckoning. And all those dogs, or least many of the big ones, got caught.

Woof.

Woof.

Woof.

Woof.

(No offense to Noah Wiley.)

The media called it "the Weinstein effect." I call it "fucking finally." After investigative reporter Ronan Farrow and the *New Yorker* dropped a bombshell, news of Hollywood heavyweights' sexual harassment and assault of women zoomed to the top of the home page.

From Harvey Weinstein to Louis C.K. to Matt Lauer, men lost their jobs and their power. They were publicly outed and ousted, revealing that women face unimaginable circumstances in the workplace. If you're anything like me, the news made you question the time(s) in your twenties when someone harassed you and you said nothing. You got mad at yourself for being too young or too scared to speak up. Mad for not knowing. Mad for knowing better and turning the other cheek anyway. Only to have that cheek grabbed by a guy on a power trip.

But in 2017, women took to their social accounts. They turned to the news. They turned to each other. The whisper network turned into a roar. The #TimesUp movement, launched by women like Reese Witherspoon, America Ferrera, Tracee Ellis Ross, Oprah Winfrey, Natalie Portman, and Kerry Washington, featured women across arenas taking the mic to share their experiences of pervasive harassment. In January 2018, almost every woman wore black to the Golden Globes in solidarity. Women everywhere called #TimesUp on men behaving badly. And together women ousted some of the most powerful men in Hollywood and media. And all of the "jokes" about "not being alone in a room with him"—*ha. ha. poke. poke.*—suddenly became not so funny.

Actress and producer Salma Hayek penned a breathtaking piece in the *New York Times* called "Harvey Weinstein Is My Monster Too." It chronicled her painful professional relationship with the producer while attempting to get *Frida*, the 2002 American biopic about the professional and private life of the surrealist Mexican painter Frida Kahlo, produced. According to Salma, he so thoroughly abused his position of power that it fundamentally altered her art. The piece was difficult to process. No, he didn't rape her. But she says he threatened to kill her. And he blackmailed her into filming a gratuitous lesbian sex scene in the movie. There is nothing funny about it.

In fact, there has never been anything funny about abuse of power and sexual assault. But in the early 2000s, when no one was talking about sexual harassment in the workplace, it somehow felt easier to laugh it off and run out of the room.

The things that I used to laugh off horrify me now. I've dealt with sexism, ageism, jerks on the way up and the way down. In elevators, at lunch meetings, and across boardroom tables. And for the most part, I, like many other women, stayed silent. I told friends, but not higher-ups.

Now I'm telling you. It was my first time traveling for work. A top executive of the company and I took a train to New England, had the client meeting, and then got dinner at a very fancy steak house. It was my first time drinking with an older male colleague. Hell, it was my first time having dinner with an older colleague. During that dinner I had two glasses of wine. That felt weird but exciting and adult-ish. I remember walking back to my hotel room. We were on the same floor, and when the elevator doors opened, I felt like making a mad dash toward my room. You know in your stomach when something is wrong or someone has some not-so-honorable intentions. The walk toward our rooms felt endless. His room was slightly farther down the hall than mine, and he paused at my door. He leaned in. Asked to come in. I could smell our dinner on his breath. My face was hot. Tears were forming. "I don't think that's a good idea," I blurted out. I scrambled to find the card swipe and rushed inside, all the blood leaving my head. He didn't press the issue, but I knew it was wrong. On top of it, he was married.

And it never went away. That tension and uncomfortableness lingered in that job until I eventually left. He called me after I quit and asked if it was because of him. I lied and said no. (Of course it was!) That experience, and all subsequent working experiences with him, had tainted my relationship to my job. I couldn't get comfortable again. Even though he apologized, I couldn't help but feel like he never should have put me in that position in the first place.

Even though one in four women in the United States reports experiencing sexism in the workplace, many incidents go unreported. Women fear losing their jobs or being seen as difficult, or think that a lawsuit will prevent them from securing another position. Women in high-level positions don't report harassment, especially when they work for larger companies, because they don't want the information to go public. Similarly, large corporations often settle in mediation to avoid public shaming of the company name. Some companies have employees sign arbitration agreements upon hiring so that any future legal matters are handled privately.

We've all been there. A senior-level executive dismisses you as "sweetie" or one of your male employees refers to you as his colleague when you are very much his boss.

There is always stereotyping in business, as in life. Sarah Kunst, venture capitalist, entrepreneur, author, and all-around badass, spoke with the *New York Times* about harassment in the tech world and trying to get her business funded. The *Times* reported, "In 2014, Sarah Kunst, 31, an entrepreneur, said she discussed a potential job at 500 Startups, a start-up incubator in San Francisco. During the recruiting process, Mr. McClure, a founder of 500 Startups and an investor, sent her a Facebook message that read in part, 'I was getting confused figuring out whether to hire you or hit on you.'

"Ms. Kunst, who now runs a fitness start-up, said she declined Mr. McClure's advance. When she later discussed the message with one of Mr. McClure's colleagues, she said 500 Startups ended its conversations with her."

She's dealt with her fair share of jerks, as have most female founders and women who are sitting across the table from mostly male, mostly white venture capitalists.

But in 2016, when Sarah spoke at C&C, she told us the following: "My work is building a billion-dollar company in the sports, fitness, and content space. That I do that as a black female founder may make me an outlier in an overwhelmingly white male tech world, but it doesn't change my mission or discourage me. It's kind of cool to beat the odds and know that my success will only help pave the way for more women like me."

She continued: "If we ask people to silo themselves—to not like a certain kind of music or dress a certain way or be a certain thing because we assume that their résumé or race precludes them from certain interests or traits, we're being close-minded and shallow. Close-minded and shallow people rarely change the world for the better.

"Be open-minded and don't be afraid to go deep. Don't assume to know where someone else 'intersects' and what drives them. Ask. If we remind ourselves that everyone we meet has intersects that we'd never expect, it's a lot easier to remain open to the new ideas and innovation they bring. To think that we're a sum of our demographic qualifiers devalues all of us."

So let's keep betting on ourselves and speaking up. Our self-worth and dignity is never something that needs to be negotiated.

Wondering just how to do that? Let's run through some scenarios and practical ways to deal with harassment in the workplace.

✦ Should You Confront the Perp?

It's not your responsibility to teach anyone a lesson. But if you think standing up for yourself is the right move and shows that you can stand your ground professionally and personally, one of the best approaches is to ask the harasser to repeat what they said. The act of making someone repeat a joke or a comment and making clear that you don't find it funny is sometimes enough to make it stop. So you could try a simple "What was that?"

There are some fires that can be put out without dragging your boss into the mix. If confronting the situation head-on is not working, it's time to take next steps.

✦ Screengrab That Shit

If you are experiencing overt or subtle sexism in the workplace, and you know a conversation or confrontation will only make it worse, start tracking it. If you are experiencing workplace harassment, or more, that makes you uncomfortable, you don't have to lie to kick it with your coworkers, meaning don't let the peer pressure, or fear of being the one employee who doesn't find it funny, stop you from tracking incidents. The sexual harassment suits that are taken the most seriously are those with the most data to back them up.

✦ Being Afraid to Report Is Normal. But Report It.

Report it to a supervisor you trust. If you work for a company that is large enough to have an HR department, take it to them. I know this is scary and that you're worried about losing your job. But ask yourself two very important questions: (1) Is any job worth feeling that uncomfortable? (2) Do you want to work for a company that doesn't take harassment complaints seriously? If they are willing to overlook and dismiss concerns of this nature, you can be sure that they do not value you as an employee. And as Samantha Bee said, "Treat every woman like she has the *New York Times* on speed dial." We aren't putting up with this shit anymore.

✦ What Happens If You're Stonewalled?

The reality is, many women who work in both the private and public sectors have experienced sexism in the workplace. Part of the issue is that all companies outwardly profess support of women in the workplace and zero-tolerance policies regarding sexual harassment and discrimination. Behind closed company doors, though, it can be a little different. If your concerns are going unaddressed and no disciplinary actions are taken, it's time to talk to an attorney. An employer may be held liable for the conduct of the employee if the employer knew or should have known of the employee's conduct and failed to take prompt remedial actions. The complaint should be made in person and in writing, and you should keep a copy for your own records. In the complaint, use the log you've created to state specific acts and dates and what effects the harassment is having on your job performance.

Note: States have varying time limits on how far from the date of incident the lawsuit can be filed. You will also need to file with the federal government. You have three hundred days to do this. Most lawyers' fees come from a percentage of your settlement or verdict. For more information on sexual harassment, visit the US Equal Employment Opportunity Commission to read the Policy Guidance Documents Related to Sexual Harassment. You can do this.

The Fine Art of Contract Negotiation

Contract and salary negotiations make a lot of us uncomfortable, to the point that we often sign the first deal we're offered. Or never negotiate the terms of our employment at all. (Guilty as charged.)

How many contracts have you signed without reading? Or without understanding the full breadth of what you're signing? (Hands up. We've all done it. That print is very fine and the language is very

formal. Also! The majority of millennial women have never negoti-ated their contract and accepted the first offer they were given.)

Tip one: Never sign the first offer you are given. If you do, you're leaving money on the table. Don't do that! Take that money off the table. At worst, you've opened up the conversation.

Tip two: Always put it in your contract that you can renegotiate your salary every six months. There are a lot of studies that show that women don't negotiate their salaries and contracts. The reasoning varies. Women aren't assertive. They don't ask. They aren't trained to ask. Women who do ask are perceived as less nice than their counterparts. At this point you've likely heard it all.

A good friend and cofounder of a highly successful streetwear brand corroborated some of this evidence with some tales from his office. "The men at my company ask for raises all the time," he shared. "When they deserve it, when they don't deserve it; they are always asking. But the women never ask." To the point where he called one of his female employees into his office to ask her, "Why aren't you asking for a raise? Do you not think you're doing great work? Do you not think you deserve one?" The employee replied that she did, but that she had been too timid to ask. "I almost want to start putting in contracts that people have to ask for raises every six months or they get fired. They have to come in prepared, and I might say no, but they have to ask." And there it is: If you don't ask for money, you won't get it.

Reddit, the social networking and news site, took a different approach. In 2015, Ellen Pao, the former CEO of Reddit, revealed in an interview with the *Wall Street Journal* that in an effort to create an "equal opportunity environment for everyone" at the company, Reddit would no longer negotiate salary with job candidates. "We come up with an offer that we think is fair," Pao explained to *WSJ*. "If you want more equity, we'll let you swap a little bit of cash salary for equity, but we aren't going to reward people who are better negotiators with more compensation." Pao told *WSJ*, "Men negotiate harder than women do, and sometimes women get penalized when they do negotiate."

Though the interim CEO stepped down from her role in 2015, she was no stranger to workplace gender discrimination herself. The tech maven gained national attention as the plaintiff in a high-profile gender-discrimination case against Kleiner Perkins, a prominent VC in Silicon Valley. Pao lost that case, but her public battle opened the floodgates about lack of gender equality in tech. Sort of like one step back, one and a half steps forward.

Neither approach is necessarily right. You can't force people to ask for a raise, and you can't tell people they can't negotiate. Neither absolute solves the problem at hand: that women don't advance at the rate men do. As usual, the best way forward is straight down the middle. Women should ask for more, and they should do so on their own terms.

So! What do those nitty-gritty terms look like?

Knowledge Is Power

Go into your negotiation with as much background knowledge as possible. This means you have to do your research! If you have a meeting with your boss about a raise, investigate what others in your position are earning in the market. If you're negotiating a project fee, know the market rate for that particular type of work. Don't be afraid to ask your friends and fellow entrepreneurs. You will sigh with relief when you know you are on the right track or, perhaps, feel a knot in your stomach when you realize you haven't been charging enough. Remember that everyone has a fucked-up relationship with money, and if we can normalize it a bit, we're doing ourselves (and our gender) a service.

Likewise, know what you're bringing to the table. Anticipate some of the more challenging questions that may arise and know how you're going to handle them. Practice tip: Put yourself in the other side's shoes. What would they want to know? What concerns might they have?

Understand Your Nonnegotiables

Have a bottom line, but be flexible. It's not a contradiction, I swear.

Is health insurance a must? Are you willing to give up working from home if your salary is higher? What are your trade-offs? Can you bring your therapy dog to work? And what's a number you have to walk away from and/or be willing to accept?

Here are some questions you should ask yourself before a negotiation meeting:

Is your position specialized? Did you need special training to qualify for the position?

If you're not in a specialized position, is there room for growth in your career?

How much money do you need to make to cover your monthly expenses?

How much money do you want to be able to save each month/year?

How much money does the average person in your job/region make? (Consult the Bureau of Labor Statistics. Also Glassdoor is a classic online resource.)

Are you willing to accept a (still realistic) lower salary to take a job that you love or one that will provide you a lot of experience? Is investing in experience going to create a bigger return in the future?

And, if so, are there areas that you can cut back on your spending in order to accommodate for this?

If you have the answers to those questions, it will be much easier to be more flexible in a meeting. Things can easily change during a negotiation, and instead of cutting off your paycheck to spite your ego, take a beat and accept that perhaps the bottom line you originally established is not realistic. You need to consider all angles before you consider walking away.

Because once that door slams, it won't open again.

Get Familiar with Negotiation Practices

If studies show that women aren't as good at negotiations, get good. Twenty percent of adult women say they never negotiate at all, even when it may be appropriate. Remember at the beginning of the book when I told you, "You aren't good or bad at anything you haven't tried"? The same applies to contract negotiations.

Slightly more frustrating, women enter negotiations with pessimistic expectations about what wage increases are available, and thus if they do negotiate, they don't ask for much: 30 percent less than men. It's time to throw a changeup. Let's ask for 30 percent more. That's called hardball, and I'm not talking about the Keanu Reeves film classic.

We might just end up with equal wages this way. Here's how:

Alex LoCasto, an attorney and founder of the Fashion Brief, focuses her practice on business litigation and dispute resolution. She says that there are two types of negotiation, and that it's important to understand both of them.

Alex explains, "There are two types of negotiation: distributive, a.k.a. positional, and integrative, a.k.a. interest-based. Positional is a win-lose mentality—there is one pizza, and we are splitting it. Interest-based is a win-win mentality—there is one pizza, and we are enlarging it. People tend to engage in positional negotiation, especially if they are on opposite sides of an issue. However, using an interest-based approach increases the chance of success for both sides." (And who doesn't want a bigger pizza?!)

The key in interest-based negotiation is identifying the other side's interests. The easiest way to do this is to simply ask, "Why?"

For example, two little girls are having a fight over an orange. Both girls take the position that they want the whole orange. If their mom cuts the orange in half and gives half to each little girl, she would be using a distributive approach. But the mom decides to ask each little girl why she wants the whole orange. Girl A tells the mom that she just loves oranges and she wants to eat it. Girl B says she wants the orange peel to use in baking some cookies. The mom gives the whole orange to Girl A, Girl B gets the whole orange peel, and both girls are happy.

By simply asking the girls *why* they wanted the orange, the mom was able to ascertain each girl's respective interests and realize that their interests did not conflict.

So let's break down how you can approach the most common workplace negotiations sans fruit or baking analogies.

1. Negotiating Your Initial Contract

   a. Not all negotiation is money. Work from home, bonus structure, and everything else is incorporated in the discussion, which is why having a flexible bottom line is important.

b. If your salary didn't hit the range you wanted, ask if there is room for commission or benchmarks you can hit to receive bonuses along the way. All of these things are fair game.

c. A press release is worth a thousand words, and raising your profile can be a powerful tool. Negotiate into your contract that you can have public relations support, speaking opportunities pitched on your behalf, and general public awareness about your personal career brand.

d. Understanding your KPIs is crucial to walking away happy. It would be prudent to have those KPIs spelled out crystal clear when you take a job. That way you know what you should be measuring.

2. Negotiating a Raise

a. Your initial contract should include the ability to renegotiate your salary at six months. This is enough time to prove your value to the company.

b. You can use back-end numbers to prove your worth. For example, if you grew your company's Instagram, track it. If page views on the site went up, track those.

c. A raise is a numbers game, literally, but like your salary, not all negotiation is about money. If a pay bump is not on the table, consider asking for a title upgrade. It shows initiative and growth within your role. Neither of those characteristics will be overlooked by a good employer. If you choose to leave your position, it is also incredibly beneficial to show a potential new employer that you can grow within a company.

d. Your initial contract should outline your performance, but it's not on anyone except you to figure out the how, what, why, when, and where of it all. If you want a raise, you should understand what the next level of performance looks like. Do some research, and be ready to show how and why you're going to take it to the next level.

3. Know Your Value and Trust in That Knowing

This isn't *exactly* part of your contract negotiation, but to get the best deal for yourself, you have to make a deal *with* yourself: Trust in your value.

Your value is multifaceted. There is the value you bring a company and the value you save a company. So when you come to the table, you should be able to understand both. Some people say that it's hard as a creative to know what kind of dollars you bring to the table. How do you put a dollar value on branding? More so, how do you put a dollar value on an idea?

For starters, creatives highly undervalue their work. If you're a creative (as in, you get paid for a creative output), you need to double your price. No company can survive without ideas. TRUST IN THAT.

But also, if you don't have the answer, don't be afraid to ask questions. You don't have to fake it till you make it—you have to deliver. Sometimes (a lot of times) that means you won't have the answer. Meeting expectations starts with understanding what you're delivering. This isn't grade school, and you don't need to be afraid to ask your question in front of the class. When companies ask you if you have any questions, let me be blunt: You. Should. Always. Have. Questions.

If you hear yourself saying, "No, I think I understand everything," it's a clear sign that you don't. Asking the right questions in both an interview and a review meeting is crucial. Would you go to lunch with a friend and not have any questions? Would you fail to contribute to the conversation? Of course not. It would appear as if you weren't paying close enough attention to have any questions.

Make sure you do your research—on the owner, on the employees, on the role—and then ask questions.

We all learn as we go, often from someone else. Your value doesn't diminish because you have to ask. You make yourself less valuable by not asking. *Mic drop.*

The more you know, the more you make.

A Different Kind of Negotiation

This brings up to a different kind of negotiation—the kind you will have with a client if you freelance or run a biz.

Negotiating with a Client

    a. Know your bottom lines. What are you willing to walk away from and what are you willing to take from a financial perspective?

b. Go in high, with a number that almost makes you feel like you want to barf, but leave room for negotiation.

c. Be on the lookout for scope creep, or the client agreeing to pay you your fee but then sneakily adding in lots of additional items on top of what was agreed to.

d. Make sure the payment terms are clear and fair, and be on the lookout for loose wording or anything that isn't specific, like "payment upon satisfaction of client." Oh hell no, that is far too vague. Know your performance metrics.

Get Familiar with the Meaning of These Clauses

So maybe you're not a traditional employee. Let's say you're a freelancer or you render services as a small business owner and you are freaked out by legal jargon.

It's the worst when you don't understand it, but it's the best because a good contract will protect you. Your contract doesn't need to be mean and scary. You just have to get past its pretentious exterior and get to know it, like any good nerd. There are numerous clauses that you should understand before signing on the dotted line and letting that ink dry.

◆ Indemnity Clauses
   In short, these allow parties to seek reimbursements or damages for certain conduct or occurrences. For example, if you are creating content (e.g., an Instagram takeover)

for someone else, that party may want reimbursement from you in the event that the content you create causes them to be involved in a copyright-infringement lawsuit. These clauses can be mutual (going both ways) or unilateral (just going to one party); you will always want them to be mutual or in your direction.

+ Confidentiality and NDAs
Confidentiality and NDAs are great ways to protect your ideas or processes, but beware of slippery language that (1) doesn't let you talk about the work you did for the client, or (2) doesn't protect your IP from being used by the other party.

+ Fee Structure
There are many different ways to structure payment: retainers, deposits, percentages. In my opinion, an up-front fee (like a 50 percent deposit) works best for things like project fees or one-off payments, whereas retainers typically fall in line with a monthly payment. Here is the kicker, though: Ask about NET PAYMENT TERMS. Many large companies have net payment terms of up to 120 days—that's four months—which means your cash flow (especially if you have employees) is going to be light AF. Often, large companies will offer programs to pay you early if they can pay with a credit card (though you will likely lose out on that credit card fee). I would suggest always pushing for net thirty (this is standard) for most clients. As an aside, be sure to build late-fee penalties into your contract, typically 5 percent for a month overdue and 2 percent every month thereafter.

+ Kill Fees

Without a kill fee, you get killed. This has saved me many times. KILL FEE! Things happen, projects fall through, events get canceled, but what doesn't have to happen is you getting screwed on the other end. I suggest building in a kill fee basically stating that if this project gets canceled for any reason other than force majeure, you are entitled to a fee (and that fee can be 50 percent or sometimes more).

+ Termination

Never a fun topic, but you want termination clauses to work both ways. I typically recommend a thirty-day out on both ends. This ensures you time to figure out your next move, and on the flip side lets you get out of a relationship you might not want to be in.

+ Cure Period

This is the period in which you are allotted to cure a "breach" of contract. A good example of this is, say, your contract doesn't allow for your company to bring on freelancers to help on a client's projects. However, you end up bringing a freelancer on, and that person ends up working on a project and the client finds out. Once they inform you they know, you can offer to "cure the breach" and move a full-time employee onto that account. Breach periods range from days to months but are important to have so you can quickly fix any issues.

+ Arbitration Provisions

These authorize a private judge to determine a dispute

between the parties. Meaning, instead of going to court, the case could be mediated by a private judge instead. Arbitration has pros and cons. For example, it can be more expensive to go with a private judge, as you will be paying for the judge's time (outside of arbitration, you are merely paying filing fees); however, it can be quicker and the dispute will not necessarily be made public (normally, all filings in a lawsuit are a matter of public record).

✦ Forum Selection and Choice of Law Clauses
These determine where and which laws will apply to any disputes. Say you're in California, but the company you're working with is based in Texas—this clause would determine which state law would apply and where any disputes would be handled. Generally, you would want to have your state's law apply and be able to handle any disputes in a place that is easily accessible to you to keep costs down. However, there may be reasons that you would want another state's law to apply. For example, California law prohibits employers from using noncompete clauses for employees.

✦ Governing Law
This is where a trial would be held and where your lawyer would need to be bar certified.

✦ Integration Clauses
These make any precontract discussions irrelevant if the contract outlines different terms. For example, say that during negotiations, there was some discussion that you would be paid extra for any work you did on weekends.

However, the contract simply states one standard rate. The integration clause would prevent those prior discussions from being considered by a judge if there was a dispute that went to court.

If you find yourself lost in legal jargon, make sure to do your research on the web, or grab a book that introduces you to basic contract provisions. And better yet, consult a lawyer. Lawyers are better than Google or Siri at looking at the law within the context of your situation. Fees to have a professional look over a contract vary, but it is worth pursuing, especially for big jobs. Bottom line: Know what you're signing, even if you think it's not important!

Finally, if you're not completely comfortable with the agreement, then *don't sign it*. Always know what you're getting yourself into, and never be too intimidated to ask questions (or if you are, send your question to me)! A good contract should spell out exactly what is expected of both parties (deliverables, deadlines, usage rights, etc.) and will protect both sides in the event of a dispute.

I would challenge you to go through each type of negotiation I laid out, think about your relationship to each and the concessions you've made along your career journey, and then use the information to make a couple of changes.

Remember: Never take the first offer.

Write down some negotiation goals for this year (work) and follow through (party).

chapter ten

Getting Paid Is Her Forte

There are a few more big negotiations, and we haven't mentioned some of the hardest yet, namely knowing when to shut down your business, when to raise money, and—on a more positive note—how and when to sell your company.

If selling feels miles away, don't feel discouraged that you're not at that point yet. It took me more than a decade to understand when it was time to sell. It's a big question!

And remember, if your dreams are big enough, it might take you your entire life to achieve them. There's no shame in that game.

FACT: There is no constant.

OPINION: Innovation is queen.

OPINION: Career paths no longer exist. It's a DIY world, and by 2020, it's projected that 50 percent of the workforce will be composed of freelancers. The future looks a hell of a lot like a 1099 tax form and a competitive creative landscape.

The good news here is that you are the captain of your own career. The bad news (with a silver lining) is that you are going to have a lot more jobs than your parents or their parents. The average millennial will now change jobs an average of four times in their first decade out of college, compared to about two job changes by Gen Xers in their first decade out of college. And that study (done by LinkedIn) is solely looking at college graduates! It's not even factoring in those who hustle outside of the traditional career structure.

FACT: The only way to battle career uncertainty is to always be innovating, and to always be looking ahead.

At some point you're going to have to change direction.

At this point in the book, you may or may not be wondering what happened to my first company, Serious Business Venture 1.0, the one I had started with Amanda. When I left that story, Create & Cultivate was on the upswing and growing quickly, and I had taken on a business partner and was hiring staff. So while I was playing Create & Cultivate cheerleader on nights and weekends and early mornings, I was also still running Serious Business Venture 1.0, which had four employees and a steady stream of large-name clients. While it felt like I had that business down pat, and like I could do marketing, events, and brand strategy in my sleep, Create & Cultivate was growing. It was growing steadily and it was like the Wild Wild West—a new and different business, something I didn't know how to do in my sleep (and still don't). I had employees on both sides of the coin working hard but also feeling neglected, not to mention that my energy and time were getting spread thinner and thinner.

Here's the thing: Work hard, but you have to know your limits.

Mentally and physically, I was exhausted, the work wasn't slowing down, and I was working nearly hundred-hour weeks every week for months. I needed help and a plan, and I wasn't quite sure what that was.

About seven months before this moment/meltdown, I had met with the PR firm Small Girls PR in New York, which had been interested in expanding to the West Coast. They were female-owned and had around thirty-plus employees and household-name clients. Years prior, we had met and shared kismet stories of starting our companies. We shared a similar brand ethos and had known and referred business to each other over the years.

Now, amid the turmoil of two companies I cared desperately about, I realized I needed help. I needed support. I needed to devote myself to my budding business that scared but excited me and slowly say good-bye to the company that had catalyzed it all.

The old adage "Timing is everything" is true. Small Girls PR's two mega-smart mega-driven cofounders and I had been in contact for years, but until our meeting a few months back, the notion that we could merge into one superior company hadn't crossed my mind. We had been business BFFs, but the more we talked about it on a cloudy New York afternoon over cocktails, the more it made sense. We could join forces. We talked about what our dream partnership could look like and how it could take shape—as a merger or an acquisition. I left the meeting feeling rejuvenated, nervous, excited, and hopeful.

But time has a funny way of slipping away.

We lost track of the conversation. Sometimes even the most exciting meetings and conversations fade away or go into hibernation (not dissimilar to dating). People get busy, fire drills happen. Life happens. Months went by.

Then, an email.

An email that changed the trajectory of everything.

pause

Let's all take a moment to remember that life can change in an instant. You can't predict when you will get a phone call, a letter, a text, an email, or a small note via carrier pigeon that alters your future. Let's all remember that life-changing news happens completely at random, and sometimes when the stars align, you get an email that you didn't know you wanted (or needed) to receive so very badly. Be ready to leap when opportunity knocks.

A single email set into motion the acquisition of Serious Business Venture 1.0.

I can fast-forward through the conversations that ensued: I sold the marketing agency to Small Girls PR as they expanded their West Coast presence. It was a long and arduous process (due diligence is no joke), but it was the best thing for my business. My clients and employees would have more resources, more support, and more infrastructure than what I was providing. Quite frankly, that sale was seven years in the making and marked the end of the era, not only financially but as a happy ending for everyone involved. The decision didn't come without much hesitation, months of negotiation, and emotions of the mixed variety. I was giving up my baby I had gone through hell to build. Make no mistake, business is personal, especially when it's yours.

At that point, it was a leap of faith. I wrote a check for $50,000 to Create & Cultivate and started trying to make this once side hustle into a business that worked and made money full-time. I was on the other side now, the brand that needed to be marketed, talked about, branded, and built up.

But look, making the decision to merge, sell, or be acquired is never easy, but here are a few key terms to know and some reasons why you should.

+ Due Diligence
  Defined as the research and analysis of a company or organization done in preparation for a business transaction, due diligence also translates to vetting the shit out of your financials year over year for the entirety of your company. Every invoice, every tax return, every stone turned.

+ Merger
  A merger usually involves combining two companies into a single larger company. The combination of the two companies involves a transfer of ownership, either through a stock swap or a cash payment between the two companies. This is typical when two companies have equal power, strength, and reach and feel they can do more together than they can separately.

+ Acquisition
  An acquisition is a corporate action in which a company buys most, if not all, of another firm's ownership stakes to assume control of it. An acquisition occurs when a buying company obtains more than 50 percent ownership in a company.

✦ Asset Sale

Typically done when a business isn't incorporated or doesn't have shares to give. You tally up your assets, including accounts receivable, technology, and goodwill (which is the hardest thing of all to calculate!), as part of the sale. "Goodwill" is code for "brand equity," or how valuable your brand is based on its public perception and, as we like to say, "buzz" and the number assigned to it.

As I said before, do not fret if you are nowhere near selling your business or have no plans to—this isn't the path for everyone. But on the other side of the coin, you don't want to be the person who waits too long to sell and is left holding onto a melting ice cream cone. Sure, it was sweet to start. But after a couple of hot hours in the sun and some enjoyment, all you have is a mess all over your hands. So, how do you know the when, why, where, and HOW MUCH of the "sale" of it all?

Experts, of course. You need to turn to the people who understand business from the inside out. Those people aren't always the most obvious. They aren't necessarily the ones gracing magazine covers and talking to the media about how they're going to change history. They are changing everything—slowly and with much calculation. Behind-the-scenes style. They may not be household names, but they move big business and generate big dollars.

Enter Raina Penchansky, CEO and founder of Digital Brand Architects, the first-to-market talent agency for the digital starlets we know and love.

In 2010, Raina played a key role in the emerging influencer market, noticing that influencers and brands didn't yet know how to work with each other. She knew there was room to be the go-between. To manage the deals. Prior to starting DBA, Raina had joined Coach in 2002, leading the exploding brand's global communications strategies for celebrity initiatives. In that role, she proved her talent for synergizing the forces of marketing, events, and public relations, becoming an instrumental force in growing the company to a multibillion-dollar brand. Under Raina's direction, Coach enjoyed a completely revitalized image through key collaborations, directional events, and strong positioning in the marketplace.

"When thinking about selling your company," she says, "you have to separate money from the equation."

Let's break that down. When you have the opportunity to sell, you should remove money from the equation. You're probably thinking, *Wait, what? Then why sell?* Raina says, "If you love what you do every day, maybe selling your company isn't the greatest idea. You have to think what you're going to do after that, what's your next step."

The BIG dream is that we all want a billion-dollar valuation.

Let's define that in hard terms. A business valuation is the process used to estimate the value of your company. It's not an exact science; Einstein unfortunately didn't create a mathematical equation to perfectly sum it up. For young business owners, however, it is crucial that you understand the value of your company, and the underlying economics of your business, especially if the time arrives to bang down investor doors.

Your company might work on your terms, but the valuation game is on the investors' terms (and they have home court advantage).

A very simple way to understand the company's worth is through asset valuation. There are five main factors to take into consideration when adding it all up, and I know you guys love a good list, so here goes:

1. Physical Assets

This includes everything from the computers to the furniture. Easy, right?

2. Intellectual Property

Patents, trademarks, incorporation papers, a website. It's all valuable. Slightly harder.

3. Owner(s) and Employees

A company's most valuable asset is in the people, both metaphorically and literally.

4. Customers/Following

Every single person who follows you, subscribes to your newsletters, or attends your conference, for instance. Getting people to pay attention to a company is almost impossible, so for those who succeed, it's very valuable. It means you've created something worth paying attention to. Remember when Instagram generated zero dollars but was worth billions? Yeah, that.

5. Recurring Revenue

Anything that doesn't have to be resold every period. Steady income streams are very enticing to investors.

There are, of course, other factors that need to be taken into consideration—the market, for instance, and if you have a stronghold on a corner of said market. That's also a numbers game, but one that's actually hard to put a number on.

But back to billion-dollar valuations.

We want to sell for stroll-off-into-the-sunset type money. The business world calls these companies the "unicorns"—private companies valued at $1 billion or more. The billion-dollar startup tech company used to be the stuff of lore. Now, we often hear about privately held companies, like Uber, Airbnb, and Spotify, being valued at over a billion dollars.

But not everyone is going to get there—nor should they.

So how do you know that it is a good time to sell? Raina says, "It's time to sell when you can see your next chapter. If you can envision doing something else for yourself, it's definitely time to sell. You have to ask yourself, 'What more can I do?' It's not about the number." In my case, I saw the next step but also had a very healthy business and knew it had value and simply needed a new home.

If you sell, you have to consider that you will most likely remain an employee of your company. In almost all circumstances, once you sell your company, you are an employee for approximately three to five years. "There are always negotiations and outliers to that standard," Raina says. But "once you sell, there is typically an onus on you to stay on board and help transition."

After that contract is up, you are typically bound by a noncompete clause, which usually ranges between six months to one year. But most business owners don't sell their company to then go start an identical company. "If you sell your company, you aren't going to do the exact same thing," Raina says. "Otherwise, why sell?" Which circles back to her initial advice: It's time to sell when you can see your next step. The next big idea. Maybe that idea is already forming, and you feel in your gut that something is about to happen. You have to be willing and able to take a step back and answer the question "What is my business and, more importantly, am I content with where I am right now?"

And in either situation, there needs to be a vision for how the company is going to scale. Should you go on a vision quest? Maybe. Might be fun. But what isn't fun is getting caught up in the dollar signs of it all. Especially because venture capitalists all talk in hundreds of millions of dollars on purpose. "It's like monopoly money," says Raina. "They love to talk in *billions* of dollars. Many VCs don't even want to talk to you unless you've got plans for a billion-dollar exit."

They like big funds and they love to lie. So come on. How many of us will get there? How many of us want to? Do you know how much you have to *make* when you take on the kind of funding that builds a billion-dollar biz?

Whoa, billions. I know this is heavy, but you have to consider what you want your company to be and what the potential is. My first company was a marketing agency, so no, I didn't have a billion-dollar exit.

And honestly? No thanks. And that's OK to say. The media likes to cover sexy numbers. Headlines champion the Evan Spiegels of the world, Facebook's $3 billion Snapchat bid, or who's tracking to go public. Behind the scenes, no one is *truly* diving into pools of cash.

Contrary and *prayer hands* to the above, not every investor is looking purely at dollar signs or annual margins. Many look at your brand equity or what aspects of your business would be extremely laborious or timely to duplicate. Investors know that they can bring scale, infrastructure, and revenue to a business. It's the special sauce—your brand equity, your community, your prowess—that cannot be replicated. *That's* where the highest value is.

Now, I mentioned that I initially put a capital contribution of $50,000 into Create & Cultivate, which makes us a self-funded company. But you can't skip a rock these days without hitting a company that has venture funding or investors. When you read that someone has raised $32 million or has billion-dollar valuations, you might want to take a step back and wonder, why do these people need all that money? I know, I know, as a small business owner it sounds extremely enticing, money for equity. Not a bad bet, right? Well, there are a lot of promises and metrics that go with that check you just cashed.

Why Raise Money?

You are building a product that requires money and scale and capital up front. For instance, Rent the Runway, a disruptive e-commerce business with a mission to democratize luxury fashion in the US, provides millions of women the ability to rent designer dresses and accessories for a fraction of the retail price. Genius idea! But imagine starting this company with no money! You have to think about the costs of the dresses, the shipping costs, the dry cleaning bill, the back end. This is a company that needed capital investment to kick-start the business.

When Should You *Not* Raise Money?

+ You are running out and desperately need cash.

+ You aren't planning on building your business to produce a big return (this is especially true of venture capital).

+ You're not clear on what to use the money for.

There are several ways to get the funds you need. You don't always have to go through a VC. You definitely don't have to raise $30 million—especially since that's not free money. The more you raise, the more you have to make. It's a stressful, serious decision not to take lightly.

So let's look at some other sources of business funding.

✦ Self-Funding

This is where you put up your own capital, which obviously varies. The cofounders of Tone It Up started with $3K and went from there. I started my first company with a laptop and an idea, $400 in office rent a month, and a Wi-Fi bill. It's all relative, and sometimes the biggest overhead is getting a space for your brain to think. While I was at Citysearch, I saved my money and accumulated a six-month savings cushion for the launch of Serious Business Venture 1.0. That is to say, I had six months' worth of rent saved up and pinched pennies until the dollars started to roll in. This was my situation, and as the circumstances (and my longtime habit of saving at least 15 percent of every paycheck) would have it, I was able to self-fund both of my businesses.

✦ Friends and Family

This is often the first round of investment that extends beyond yourself. This round of investment comes from, you guessed it, friends and family! Depending on who your inner circle is, this round could put you in six-figure territory and set you up to head into the angel-investment round. (Did I mention this process takes time? One step at a time.) My only warning: Your clique is probably not completely composed of savvy investors à la *Shark Tank*, and for this reason, many friends-and-family investors don't see a return. Help protect them by aligning your visions on structuring elements, vesting, share type, and general governance.

+ Crowdfunding and Kickstarter

Take it to the people. The Kickstarter model is much like the angel-investor model, except the dollars are coming from strangers who cosign your vision. *Darling* magazine, a publication near and dear to my heart (and one of our first media partners for Create & Cultivate), crowdfunded their initial production costs for their female-centric and inclusive magazine movement.

+ Traditional Small Business Loan

Not to be overlooked. The Small Business Administration is a great resource, especially for female entrepreneurs.

+ Angel Investors

Legit angels for new business owners. These are people who provide capital for a startup, most often in exchange for ownership equity or convertible debt. Convertible debt is, quite simply, a loan. The intention of convertible debt, for the investor, is to convert it into equity. Angel investors typically invest between $25K and $100K of their own money into businesses.

+ Venture Capitalist

An investor who provides startup capital to new businesses. Unlike angel investors, venture capitalists invest an average of $7 million per company. Raising venture capital takes much more time because they have a lengthy diligence process. They are willing to take large bets, but they place those bets very carefully. Taking money from a VC usually requires a serious commitment to the firm from the business owner, and a VC will often require a board seat and/or a board of directors to be formed. Simply put, if you don't need $3 million plus to start your company, you don't necessarily need a VC.

So, you need to really think: What is your business? What does your business look like with a capital investment? If you haven't realized this yet, the answers to those questions should be different. A $2 million business should not and cannot be the same as a $200 million business. And more importantly, if you have a successful company that pays you and your employees well, it's OK to be content with that. Again, don't get seduced by big numbers. Sometimes the answer is yes, you can use the money, and sometimes the answer is no, you don't need to raise funds.

Now let's dig into an idea you've likely heard a lot about: scale. "Scale" is another word the business world likes to throw around. Setting proper goals and writing a business plan is part of what scaling is all about. Nothing is harder or takes more time than growing your business. And the bigger you get, the bigger the risk that comes with it.

As they say, you have to spend money to make money. But how much money is too much money spent? You don't need to be profitable year one, but if you are still losing money by year three, that's a red flag. A big one.

That's not what we call scaling effectively. You should be growing responsibly and reinvesting smartly; while profits aren't the only point, when you're scaling effectively, the brand is evolving in a profitable direction.

But even if you don't have a billion-dollar biz or exit, or a pool of money, you will always have yourself. That's amazing news because . . .

Your Personal Brand Will Transcend Where You Work

Your brain, the hard drive inside your head that stores your intellectual property and your wildest dreams, and your brand are intertwined, after all. They have a symbiotic relationship, what with the brain creating your brand, and your brand representing your brain and its ethos.

Your brand is more than a mission or vision statement; it is a testament to what your creativity and values can build. No one can rob you of your emotional integrity or what's stored in your own head.

FACT: Your personal brand will transcend the companies you create and/or the companies you work for.

OPINION: I think the phrase "personal brand" is in need of a brand overhaul itself, having become more of a trigger or a cultural cliché than the important career step it is. I'll be the first to admit it: "Personal brand" sounds stifling and inauthentic. It sounds like a facade.

BACK TO FACTS: Our reality, as I write this, is that everyone has a personal brand. Whether you are aware of it or not, you already have one. Your brand is ever-evolving, amorphous, and intrinsic to your being. It's simply how you represent yourself to the world. It's the notion that yes, your appearance and how you put yourself together matters, but your attitude, proactivity, creativity, and output matter more. Sure, lipstick helps, but actions matter more than makeup.[*]

I believe you can boil your personal brand down with this extremely scientific questionnaire:

---

[*]Never forget that Mark Zuckerberg is lauded for wearing a uniform of jeans, a T-shirt, and a hoodie. Every. Single. Day. It's his ideas and his actions that we're intrigued by. If our male counterparts can redefine their brands in relation to the traditional workplace, so can we.

- ✦ What are the core pillars that make you unique?

- ✦ How do those pillars relate to your career?

- ✦ What do those pillars look like?

- ✦ How do you want to be seen in your career?

- ✦ How do you want to be seen outside of your career?

- ✦ How would you like others to introduce you or talk about you?

There was a point when someone said to me, "What are you, a blogger? A business owner? A conference creator?" and I genuinely was just like, *Yep, all of those things.* But I got their point. It was hard to pinpoint and peg down exactly what I was doing. It took years of finesse, as well as a very strategic rebrand from "Jackie" to "Jaclyn" and from "blogger" to "CEO," but it worked and was worthwhile.

And look, your Instagram bios do matter. Pay attention to your message and you will be rewarded, if only by being mindful about the brand you're already projecting.

chapter eleven

Take It from Them

K.
      OK.

OK.

It's been many chapters of me. My voice. My advice. Why take my word on all of this? It's always smart to get a second, third, fourth opinion.

So I did a little research with some of the brightest, most intelligent female founders rocking their WorkParty today. I spoke with all of these women about everything from being vulnerable in the workplace, to leveraging past work experience, to finding their voice, to hiring the experts.

Take it from them. I certainly did. I've met every one of these women in a different capacity. Aimee Song and I did a Levi's video campaign together in 2014. (Please don't Google. OK, fine, Google. I'm wearing some rocker bracelets and a really sad cat-eye in my one-bedroom apartment/office.) Jen Gotch and I connected over email after I stalked her weekly when she first launched Ban.do when it was just a hair-accessories line. Jen Rubio has been a friend and colleague for some time, and I was lucky enough to invest in her company, Away, after she left Warby Parker. I also stalked Jihan Zencirli, a.k.a. Geronimo, and asked for free balloons for Create & Cultivate. She said no. So I bought them. I cold-LinkedIn-requested Michelle Lee—turns out our stories are so shockingly similar, it almost seems fated that we met.

The point is, every one of these women has a story that somehow ties back into my entrepreneurial journey as well as all of yours. The second point is don't be embarrassed to reach out to women you admire. You'll never guess what you could learn. The women below graciously agreed to talk with me about their stories.

Jen Gotch on Being Vulnerable

Name: Jen Gotch
Company: Ban.do
Name of Her Game: Giving a voice (and face) to the hard stuff
Most Likely To: Survive the end of the world
Find Her: On roller skates @jengotch

On December 1, 2017, Jen Gotch, creative mastermind and founder of the beloved Ban.do, the lifestyle company that's "serious about fun," posted something equally serious on her Instagram.

Her post read:

23 years ago, when I was 23 a doctor gave me Prozac. He was trying to help. I was in a very dark place in my mind and at that particular time if you were sad and didn't hear voices you pretty much got Prozac. I felt better after I took it for quite a while and then I felt worse. A lot worse. I went into therapy and over many years met with 6 other doctors as they all tried a ton of different drug

cocktails to get me to a place where I could actually function. No one got it right. It was a scary, uncertain, lonely time for me. I felt misunderstood by everyone around me including the doctors that I was paying to help me, and that was incredibly alienating. Then a lightbulb. What if I was actually Bipolar and not just Depressed? I saw a new Doctor, he confirmed the diagnosis that my therapist and I thought and prescribed a two drug combination that changed my life. CHANGED MY LIFE!!! I stayed on those drugs for about 10 years. I got myself together. I got married, I started a company and then I stopped taking the drugs. It was an accident—I went on a 5 day trip and forgot them—but I felt fine so . . . I stopped. I felt fine for years. I was convinced my brain chemistry had changed and I could manage, but this is a common trap for people with mental illness and I fell right in.

With Andrew being gone I've had a lot of alone time. Like a lot. You watch my stories. You know! I realized I wasn't ok and I was just scared and prideful and ashamed that I hadn't miraculously risen above it. That I hadn't evolved beyond my physiology. I'm still suffering. So I'm starting to take medicine for it again. I wanted you to know because you have supported me and encouraged me and helped me realize what was going on and that it was ok. I'll keep you posted every step of the way, since I know this will be useful for so many of you that are suffering, too. Ok that's it. Side note: I know you are going to ask about my pj's and it's not because you don't care about mental illness it's just that you like rainbows as much as me. I get it. They are from Reformation, but I think they are sold out. Bye.

Wow. That's a kind of honesty that we don't typically see from founders. Talk about authenticity and vulnerability.

But back to Ban.do.

Followers tune into Jen's Instagram Stories like it's a new Netflix drop. They resonate with everyone from CEOs to twenty-two-year-old graphic designers trying to figure out their lives. Why? Because Jen is a founder unafraid to lift the curtain on the hard parts of her life.

"I never expected to be a public figure talking about mental health," she says. "For me, the worry is overpowered by the desire to get it out. To connect. To expose that depression is something experienced by a lot of people."

She's not alone. "Founder depression" is very common among female entrepreneurs, especially those convinced that they need to act the part. They don't talk about it in business school or boardrooms. And they certainly don't seem to talk about it in front of male peers. From what I've seen, they don't even like to talk about it in front of other female founders. But why?

Starting a business takes confidence. Entrepreneurship is essentially you telling the world, "Hey, listen, you need this service or this product and I am going to be the one to deliver it to you. Me. Out of the 7.125 billion people on the planet, I have the ability to solve this problem for you." That's no small undertaking. Telling someone you're depressed feels like the opposite of both confident and competent. Telling someone that being the owner of a company is the hardest, scariest-monster-under-your-bed challenge you've ever stared down? That's terrifying.

It's why Jen's commitment to truth-telling is so powerful. There have been many male startup founders who've come forward, and even those who have taken their own lives. But women have been less vocal on the matter, likely due to the fact that we're still trying to figure out how to not get harassed in the workplace. (Looking at you, 2017.)

But not Jen. And thank goodness for her. Seriously.

She says, "Some people wonder, 'Is saying all this going to look really bad?' Or, 'I can't allow investors to think I'm not stable enough to run a company.' But it's such a natural part for me. A lot of people 'compliment' me by saying, 'Oh, if you can do it, I can totally do it.' I know it's meant to be nice. But I still have thoughts of not being good enough all the time."

Most everyone, not only founders, knows what this is like. Two American psychologists, Pauline Clance and Suzanne Imes, even named it in 1978: imposter syndrome. You constantly feel like a fraud. You worry you don't have what it takes. And the more accolades you receive, the worse it can feel. You're always waiting for the bottom to drop out. Self-doubt. The fear of measuring up. The stress of rising to the next level. I've been there so many times, often too afraid to speak about it out of fear of looking weak.

Jen has found herself in the safe position of being able to speak her truth without fear of repercussion. "I'm very clear with the owner of our company about the things I suffer from. I'll tell them, I woke up and I have clinical depression today and I can't do it. In my mind it's a physiological problem."

On the day-to-day, she's likewise surrounded by incredibly supportive people, three of whom are female employees who have been with Ban.do since inception. "The girls that we hired—no one had experience. I didn't have experience," she jokes. Today the Ban.do staff is a "really diverse mix of people that are openhearted and that feels safe and good. That wasn't planned," she says. "It was energy attracting energy." It's also incredibly exciting and exhilarating to see those three initial women grow up with the company. "To see the powerhouses they've become—I don't have kids and I'm probably not going to have kids, the people at Ban.do are the closest thing to me that's something I created and put everything I had into. To watch that happen is really exciting for me."

She may not have had traditional experience, but her sense of humor has been her superpower. "Even when I was a freelancer, I wasn't the best at my job necessarily, but people always wanted me around." (*Ahem.* Reminder: Be a fucking pleasure to work with.) "Being funny and being able to make people laugh is a very powerful thing," she says.

"And honestly, if there is a strategy to any of this, it's this: I don't want anything to look that easy, whether it's personal stuff or work stuff. Because being alive is very hard and complicated. And I'm happy that I have a platform to talk about what's on my mind and push the boundaries beyond 'What's fun?!' I want to use it for positive reasons that don't feel frivolous."

Alli Webb on Dealing with Copycats

Name: Alli Webb
Company: Drybar
Name of Her Game: Changing the whole beauty game
Most Likely To: Multitask you under a table
Find Her: Blowing competition away @AlliWebb

What Alli Webb has accomplished in a few short years would make anyone's head spin. And if it's up to Alli, that head will have beautifully blown out hair.

The founder of Drybar, the nation's premier blow-dry bar specializing in just blowouts (no cuts, no color), revolutionized the hair game for busy women. After attending beauty school, Alli was traveling in her van to people's homes to give them custom blowouts. She was the first one to recognize that women needed a space where they could walk in, get a blowout, and walk out feeling fabulous. Thirty-five minutes. Forty bucks. It was genius. And the public agreed.

Drybar grew from four locations and $1.5 million in revenue in 2010 to twenty-five locations and $19 million in revenue in 2012. In 2013, Drybar reached the milestone of its 1,111,111th customer; she was awarded free blowouts for life. (Lucky.)

Head spinning yet? Of those early days, Alli says, "We knew that there was something really special here that we just kind of stumbled upon. I'd like to tell you that this was my grand plan this whole time to expand this thing as big as it is now, but it truly wasn't. I was up at night doing the math to see what we could do to make the business viable, but it was really early on that we realized we were on to something pretty amazing." You'll recall that I went through this exact feeling with Create & Cultivate. It's that magic that keeps you going.

What Alli and Drybar were onto was a full industry disruption.

She found the whitespace in the billion-dollar beauty biz, and today, Drybar, a seven-year-old company, is taking in revenue of over $70 million. Talk about lucky number sevens. They have eight-five locations.

When people talk to Alli about changing the industry, it's still a little surreal for her. "The first year into it," she says, "I was like, 'Oh shit!' We did change the industry. I thought that in a place like LA girls needed a place to get blowouts. I was really just thinking, 'Why doesn't this exist?!'"

So she thought, *Why not build this?* Her brother invested $250,000. Alli and her husband put in $50K. With those dollars, they opened the flagship Brentwood location. She wanted to build an experience that didn't look, feel, or smell like a salon. "In the back of my mind we hoped it would catch on and we would continue to grow with this. I don't think any of us knew how big the opportunities were going to be."

The opportunity was so huge that Alli has had to deal with a fair share of copycats replicating her business model. She was super sensitive about it in the beginning. "It was still new and I was very overprotective, and I definitely still am. There are those cases where people are literally taking words and exact verbiage from our website."

She says people have replicated the "10 Core Values" that Drybar bases their work around. "Things like that really kind of drive me up a wall, and it's hard to deal with." But she does deal. "There are blowout bars that have popped up in locations that we aren't in and I think that, overall, has raised awareness to the category, which is good."

But you can't replicate soul (and you can't copy someone's heart).

Lightning never strikes twice, and Drybar remains the authority in the space. "We have eighty-five locations for a reason," Alli notes. "I

"*I knew there was a hole in the market & I could fill it.*"

-ALLI WEBB

have seen a lot of these places open and close, and I can probably tell you why that has happened to most of them. I know how incredibly hard these businesses are to run."

Alli happens to be running on her toes.

"As a business owner you have to be on your toes and know what everyone is doing. Be aware, be on it, and always do your best. You can't beat hard work, even if you copy it."

Jen Rubio on Leveraging Your Corporate Know-How to Build Your Startup

Name: Jen Rubio
Company: Away (cofounder)
Name of Her Game: Making travel chic again
Most Likely To: Be on a plane
Find Her: Going up, up @away

"I'm not one of those people who always said, 'I want to be an entrepreneur.'"

Um, same.

Personally, it took me years to reconcile myself with that word.

But still, it's an interesting point from Jen Rubio, cofounder of the wildly popular travel and lifestyle brand Away. "There's a lot of people who think being an entrepreneur is really cool. But I wasn't one of them. I wasn't sitting at my desk thinking, 'When am I going to start my own company?'"

Prior to launching Away with biz partner and cofounder Stephanie Korey, Jen and Stephanie both worked at Warby Parker, and they took the lessons of a direct-to-consumer biz with them when they left. They officially launched Away in 2015.

Of her time at Warby Parker, Jen says, "On a micro level, every single day, we ask ourselves if what worked for Warby Parker would work for Away." Oftentimes, she says, that answer is no. There is no command-V (a.k.a. the paste function) in business. Sure, Away and Warby are both new, young, direct-to-consumer businesses. But that's really where the similarities end.

"What I learned from WP is that it's not as easy as copying and pasting strategy from one company to another," Jen says. "At a higher level, I learned the importance of connecting with our customer. You don't create a brand in a bubble. We are always thinking of how to better serve our customers and listen to their needs. We let those needs drive our product decisions." She says while that idea might seem obvious to young entrepreneurs, she doesn't think it's necessarily an investment in people made by corporate companies. But it's the basis of the brand: a love of travel and a love of connecting with people. Relationships and travel drive her.

Dedicated to luggage for the way "people really move" without a first-class price tag, Away set the tone with its first product: a beautiful, high-end minimalist carry-on without the zeros. At under $250, Away made traveling in style (hello, silk lining, removable laundry bag, TSA-approved lock, charging ports) a whole lot easier. *Vogue* called it "the perfect carry-on." *Forbes* 30 Under 30 took notice. Steph and Jen had accolades in the bag, but they didn't stop there.

Away is more than a luggage brand. It's a lifestyle. "The soul of what Away is comes from a genuine love of travel," Jen says. "When I think back to my earliest conversations with Steph, I was already thinking about the future of Away. I was focused on fixing everything that's terrible about travel. Curious and passionate about how we can make it better. You can build a piece of luggage and you can sell it, but my entire passion throughout my career has been to build something that people connect to emotionally. I knew we had to really build a brand to do that."

Today, two of the questions Jen asks herself are "What are we capable of doing *now*?" and "What makes the most impact?"

(You'll remember this from the four questions you should ask yourself before leaving your full-time job to focus on your side hustle.)

For Away, it all goes back to listening to their customer. "Editorial is something our customers are really looking for. It's also something we knew we could do well." Which is why Away has released a magazine and a podcast. At time of print, they've printed two hundred thousand magazines. They have tens of thousands of podcast downloads. "It's clearly something the customers wanted," Jen says. "There's a million things you can do every day, but you have to look at the intersection of opportunity and impact. And honestly, we also think about how positively it will affect our brand."

In the "retail apocalypse" era, as big-box stories are rapidly closing, Away has taken the risk on brick-and-mortar locations, transforming the doom and gloom concept into a thriving subsect of their business. Jen says, "A big misconception is that direct-to-consumer is online only. A lot of startups begin online because of the cost. It's how you can scale the fastest. But we want to be direct-to-consumer in every sense of the word. In the same way Instagram is a channel for us, we see each of our stores as a channel. Each point is an opportunity to own our story. We don't discount the importance of brick-and-mortar stores for bringing our brand to life."

And living Away is doing that. "It's getting harder and harder to connect with people. When I worked at Warby Parker, all you needed was a nice Instagram with lots of pictures. People would feel connected to your brand. But now every single brand is doing that. So how do we differentiate ourselves?" she asks. "Offline experience is one of the main ways we're determined to connect to the customer."

Sounds exactly like what we tell Create & Cultivate attendees.

Geronimo on Turning Your Passion into Profit

Name: Jihan Zencirli
Company: Geronimo Balloons
Name of Her Game: Balloon art
Most Likely To: Blow your mind
Find Her: By the helium tank @geronimo

Jihan Zencirli is the creative genius turned balloon boss behind the colorful art installations that billow up buildings and blow up your Instagram feed. She found out she was good at balloons back in 2011.

A "tad lonely child," Jihan says that she spent a majority of her youth on the floor next to her bed, with a pen, journal, magazines, and three-ring binders equipped with plastic sleeves. "I spent hours pulling out articles and images," she shares, "filing them into the binder and making lists and detailed notes of the things I wanted to do in my life, and the specific year I wanted to achieve them by." It was this early act of planning and dreaming that set her in motion. "I never made the goal of being a balloon artist. But I did plan and yearn and dream for an adult life of travel, red shoes, late bedtimes, being independent, making a living by using my hands to create—and," she adds, "dating Jimmy Fallon."

The artist acknowledges herself as her biggest challenge, in part stifled by the need to plan. And like the rest of us, she's not "above staying in bed, trolling the internet to leave snarky comments about past purchases on Amazon when I'm down in the dumps."

And yet she's captured our hearts and imaginations by turning her formative years into Geronimo. From passion to profit, it's the Jihan way since her youth. "As a child, being creative was my way of trying to fit back into the world outside of me," she says. "I would ask for creative things for gifts—if someone would give me a stack of construction paper, it made me so happy." But creativity didn't pay the bills, and over the years she had a variety of odd jobs to make ends meet.

The daughter of a single mom who taught high school, Jihan has had a hustle since her start. Convinced she had to find a way to take care of herself, she says she became a bit of a survivalist. She knew she wanted to make a living and support herself, as evidenced by one summer in Japan. "I had an aunt and uncle who lived there and I learned how to make origami and I went door to door selling origami tulips." Then she had a card company. "I look back now and I think I always knew I would take care of myself. I would sit on my bed for *hours and hours* journaling my plans."

(Side note: I'd love to see those journals.)

Those plans included having a creative way out. "In high school, we had to shadow and study a profession," she says. "I chose to shadow a donut maker. Everyone saw it as a joke, but I really wanted to understand how to be a small business owner. Not everyone becomes the architect or dentist or doctor."

She became a balloon artist.

Geronimo, as it exists today, was forged from Jihan's own interests. "I was always going to be someone who had to invent her own category," she shares. In 2009 she created her first prototype for what would become Geronimo. "I would tell my friends about the idea, and they would say, 'What? You want to do balloons?' And I would say, 'No, it's this thing that no one has experienced before. I want to share this with people.' I invented a balloon prop as a way to express how I felt about others. I love the way the balloons made people feel, and I knew I wanted to do it more."

She came to LA on a whim, but within that first week, she immediately went to work. At first, she was hand delivering her creations via a VW Bug. Every balloon installation was incredibly labor-intensive. She wasn't charging for delivery. And she was such a fresh breath of creative air that customers started inviting her in to chat. #NotATypicalLAStory.

Some friends connected her with Joy Cho, of Oh Joy!, who posted and tagged a photo of Jihan's creation. Overnight, so many people visited her "little rinky-dink site" that she woke up the next morning to $30K in her bank account from random people. *Cha-ching*.

"The balloons were a funny thing to believe in, but I felt like this was my connection to people. It became my goal, my focus. Ride or die. Let's do this. It kept bringing me joy."

And it was bringing other people joy. It brought Oh Joy! joy, clearly. And she did Jihan a solid as a result, which should serve as a reminder: Always be paying it forward. Always be building bridges, not burning them down. The favors that happen, the people who believe in you over your first years in biz, are priceless—the favor economy is real. And Oh Joy! posting that photo . . . priceless favor.

Which brings us to pricing. How do you price something that no one's ever seen before? You might think, *It's just a balloon*. Not exactly. I even remember cold-reaching-out to Jihan for one of our early Create & Cultivate conferences. I needed to have one of her creations in a photo booth—I knew it would be an instant hit. The cost was seventy-five dollars. That was a huge expense for us in the beginning, and yes, I tried to negotiate the price down. Jihan didn't budge. And honestly, props to her. She knew her value and she stuck to it. She also, I would later come to find out, needed to buy groceries.

"Truthfully," she says of the cost, "I was sort of making it up." In 2007, the friend who sold Jihan her first large balloon Skyped her and said, "Look, you need to raise your prices unless you want to live in your basement." So she tripled her prices. It didn't come from a place of greed but, rather, treating her work as an art form, something that

"took a lot of time creating and adjusting." She'd get better materials and find better quality helium. "While it may have seemed like I was 'killing it,'" she says, "I was spending a lot of money trying to make it better. I had to set the pricing with that in mind." It was also very time-consuming. She says she thought, "'If I'm only going to be able to create two today, I need to be able to pay for my groceries this week. Forget rent, let's just try to cover groceries.' So if I was to sell one for seventy-five dollars, I could pay for groceries and I could pay for gas."

She also knew and understood early on what she wanted to turn her passion into. The balloons were her way to connect with people, but they were also her career. They were beautiful and cool and . . . *hers*, and she needed the pricing to indicate as much.

"I invented a market for something that is kind of silly, but it's real," she says. "Everything has the central theme of making something for someone that will evoke a little bit of joy."

She adds, "All of the sudden I was doing things on a larger scale. And that's a growing pain on its own. I needed staff, I needed insurance, I needed a better car and to be able to meet the demands of this 'thing' that was supposed to be a one-off balloon delivery. It wasn't my intention to make it an exclusive party favor, but had I started my pricing off at something really modest, people would have looked at it as a fifteen-dollar product."

Michelle Lee on Cutting Through the Noise

Name: Michelle Lee
Company: *Allure* magazine (editor-in-chief)
Name of Her Game: Changing beauty standards
Most Likely To: Get her name on top of a masthead
Find Her: Making boomerangs @heymichellelee and bossing it up @allure

Michelle Lee has a "glamorous" job. A movie job with the kind of title that young fashion darlings are enamored by. But her path to editor-in-chief of *Allure* wasn't always red-bottom soles and front-row seats at Chanel.

Growing up in Connecticut, Michelle didn't know what she wanted to do. In fact, up until middle school, the fierce fashionista was certain that she wanted to be a baker. "Whenever anyone would ask, that's what I said," she laughs. "I don't even bake a lot."

Her sophomore year of high school, Michelle's dad lost his job and the family moved to South Florida (holler at my hometown!). Spending her last two years of high school in Fort Lauderdale was total culture shock. "In hindsight," she says, "it was the greatest thing that ever happened to me. It exposed me to so much. It got me out of my comfort zone." All useful traits in the business world. "You have to be able to adapt and meet new people."

A self-described "bored kid" in school, Michelle was eager. "I've always been an eager person. I was eager to work, eager to graduate." She went to college at University of Florida, but the future was always on her mind. Her sophomore year she chose journalism as her major. "I really like writing and I really liked the building the journalism department was in," she jokes. She ended up graduating with a very specific degree in magazine journalism, but as a result of her eagerness, she scheduled all of her classes at night and worked during the day. By her junior year, she had a full-time job as a staff writer at a Florida paper called the *Weekly Planet*. By the end of her time there, she was penning features and cover stories.

Not bad for a girl who didn't know what she wanted to do. But she also knew she wanted to get out of the state.

"Coming from Florida, you can feel very insulated there, which is great for some people," she says. "But I knew I wanted to do something more." She also knew that she needed to work incredibly hard to make it to and in New York. "I knew I didn't have the degree from Columbia, I didn't go to Harvard, but I was the hardest worker out there."

She applied for an internship as part of the American Society of

Magazine Editors. Her top choice was *Glamour*, and she got it. The editor-in-chief at the time was Ruth Whitney, and Michelle knew this was her big in. She didn't even walk in her graduation because she was so ready to head up to Manhattan to work. "I knew if I could just get my foot in the door," she says, "it would be the beginning of every-thing."

And it was. She went on to become editor-in-chief of a little glossy you might know and love, *Nylon*. In 2015, she took over for *Allure*'s famed editor Linda Wells, who had had a twenty-four-year run at the magazine. Michelle was ready to fill her shoes, and no, she didn't have the direct line to Anna Wintour either (though now she does); she had a little bit of luck, opportunity, and a lot of hard work.

"I've been editor-in-chief a couple of times now. And it's interest-ing because I was never a natural-born leader. I almost overthink and care too much about what people think about me"—especially in the beginning, she says. "There's a weird tipping point where you're a se-nior member of staff and you're everyone's colleague. And then your position changes and you have to start making decisions that make some people unhappy." The learning curve was hard for Michelle.

She eventually gave up the idea of being well liked. "If you're so concerned with making everybody happy, you're going to make nobody happy, including yourself." She figured out how to manage people in a way that maintained her own integrity, while also exerting authority. "The other tricky thing about being editor-in-chief," Michelle shares, "is that the job has changed so much in the last twenty years. I'm in the position where a portion of my time is spent on the magazine, but we also have digital. We have video. We have licensing. It's so many different things. It's the great thing about the job, but it's also the challenging part. It's hard from a time-management perspective. You have to figure out how to chop up your time adequately in a way that gives attention to all the other verticals."

So how does she handle being in constant flux? Number one, she says, is hiring and surrounding yourself with the right people. She's not a micromanager. She hires trustworthy people whom she can motivate and "let go." She spent her first year at *Allure* getting the staff right. "It's not an easy process—you have to take time and do team-building things. People get impatient and think things are going to change right away. I say it takes about six months for things to gel."

She's been hiring people for over a dozen years now. She likes to hire people based on attitude. "I think you can get a vibe off of someone early on in the interview process." She also likes people who have really, truly done their research.

And she focuses on the culture of the company: "Introducing one person in who is either toxic or doesn't gel can really mess up how the culture of the company works. If you have a cultural mix that doesn't work, you're going to be dealing with their gripes every day." True.

As for her everyday, it's not just playing with products. "Our greater mission is to redefine beauty standards. I have been in women's publishing for two decades. When I started, magazines were still writing cover lines like '11 Ways to Please Your Man' and 'Ten Ways to Lose 10 Pounds in 5 Days.' We're so much more aware of the things we say, do, and the long-lasting effects they have on women's psyches. We want to subvert the way old-school women's publishing used to do things. We don't want to be faux empowering. We want to be living what we speak."

Just last year, *Adweek* named Michelle Editor of the Year and *Allure* Magazine of the Year. "We'd been working so hard on bold statements. We had Helen Mirren on the cover, as the end of anti-aging. I really believe that if you give people a higher mission, then people will enjoy coming to work. We can write about sparkly nail polish *and* six Muslim bloggers who are changing the world."

WorkParty on to that.

Aimee Song on Being the OG of OG Bloggers

Name: Aimee Song
Company: Song of Style
Name of Her Game: Fashion blogging deal-maker, first to market
Most Likely To: Make smart, calculated decisions
Find Her: Talking to millions of people @aimeesong

Aimee Song was a pioneer. Part of the Wild Wild West of bloggers. Arguably one of the first to market. And the market responded to her.

She admits that the hardest thing about where she is now is "that I have a team, I have employees, I have brands and clients that I work with. There are a lot of legal aspects to it. Things I wasn't trained in. I don't have a business background, and trying to turn on my business brain is hard sometimes. I'm very much a creative."

But let's go back to day one for Aimee Song and Song of Style, pre millions of followers and million-dollar deals. The year was 2008. Right around the time I also launched Some Notes on Napkins. Ah, the good old days.

"I had just started my first year in college, and because I had an internship and was working two separate jobs," Aimee says, "I didn't have time to experience the college life. I was always working. So I started a blog as a hobby, a creative outlet. I didn't go to parties, so I was having fun collecting images."

But it wasn't always Song of Style as we know it today. Aimee, an interior designer by trade, wanted an interior design blog. Naturally. Makes sense. Yet it didn't entirely, at least to her, and within the first week, she transitioned it to a personal style blog. "It wasn't consistent, but I was already into fashion. I was already taking outfit photos and posting them on MySpace and Facebook and asking friends and family, 'Oh, do you like this dress?'"

So instead of going with what she was "good" at, she went with her gut. You have to be ready to go with your second idea.

And the response was good, like thousands-of-followers good, and they kept coming. She's considered one of the most successful bloggers to date. Yet in spite of brand deals and a massive following, she didn't stop pursuing her career as an interior designer. "I didn't quit my interior design career until about three years ago," Aimee says. "Even though my blog *could* provide a full-time income, and I was working full-time hours, I didn't focus fully on it until about 2014."

That's right. She didn't make the leap from side hustle to full-time until 2014. Years after storied success. And it's not because she didn't understand that it was a viable business. No, Aimee says, "I knew it was a business about a year and a half into it." But she worked crazy full-time hours on her side hustle in order to create a legitimate runway for herself.

And not the kind of runway you see her sitting front row at, but a business runway. "Runway," as defined by the startup world, is how long the business can survive if costs stay constant. (Hint: They never do if you want to grow.) On average, a small business owner should be able to cover monthly costs for eighteen months.

Working two full-time jobs is hard, but she put in the work. The hours. I know this hustle all too well. But it's why Aimee was reportedly paid $500,000 to be Laura Mercier's first digital influencer, according to *Women's Wear Daily*. If true, that's an unprecedented paycheck for a blogger to be the face of a beauty brand.

Beyond putting in the work, the influencer is incredibly savvy when it comes to dealing with competition. "A lot of people think, the more blogs there are, the harder it is to survive, but in my opinion, it's the thing that really helped. The more bloggers there were, the more seriously brands took bloggers." And by the time people started paying attention, Aimee knew she had more value than a paid ad in a magazine. (Media kit numbers exist online to anyone who wants to download them.) "So," she says, "I started charging brands."

She was one of the first, and as we all know, being first to market is always difficult.

To price herself, she did some research due diligence. She didn't have other fashion bloggers to compare rates with, and product placement was a new concept, so she compared her traffic to the interior design blogs she was following. "I remember seeing small, thumbnail-sized banner ads on their sites," she says. "Several of those blogs had their banner ad pricing listed. I knew that I got more traffic than them. So I charged the same amount—which was a couple hundred dollars. I eventually raised the price."

She also made the decision early on about who and what brands she would work with. From day one she wanted Song of Style to be a luxury brand. Which meant turning down big-money checks from brands that wouldn't fit that luxe narrative she was creating.

That meant she said no *a lot*. And still does. "I say no a lot. There's a power in saying no. When you say no, you say yes to other opportunities."

Her dream? Chanel.

"I knew that my goal was to work with Chanel. I wanted to work with Louis Vuitton. I wanted to work with heritage brands. I couldn't sacrifice working with more budget-friendly brands, no matter how good the paycheck was. As far back as I can remember, thinking about my end goal or dream partnership, I was always aware of what brands wouldn't want to work with me if they looked back and saw that I had worked with other low-budget brands."

Luckily, Aimee could say no early on because she had income from her interior design business. "I didn't have to rely on my blog for income. I always remained true to myself. Everything I do, I do out of love. I never want to be peer-pressured into something."

But everything wasn't coming up roses all the time. When she launched her blog, her then boyfriend helped her set it all up. When the relationship didn't end the way Aimee had imagined, she was left in the dark both professionally and personally. "When we broke up, I didn't know how to do anything," she says. "I didn't even have the passwords to many of my platforms. I had relied so much on him. In that moment, it made me take my website seriously. Really seriously. And I needed to find professionals I could trust. It was a good and hard lesson."

Another lesson she's learned and is happy to pass on: Don't trend-hop.

"I wasn't one of the first people to jump on Instagram. It actually took me a while. I've always taken my time. You look at other people and think, 'Oh, that person's doing that, I need to do that,' but there are no actual standards. We're all wired differently. We'll all have our moment. That's something I've always believed in, and it's helped me go at my own speed. Sometimes it works, sometimes it doesn't. But at the end of the day I'm happy."

Happy people = WorkParty.

Rebecca Minkoff on Success on Its Own Time

Name: Rebecca Minkoff
Company: Rebecca Minkoff LLC
Name of Her Game: Handbags, accessories, being a fashion icon
Most Likely To: Disrupt contemporary fashion
Find Her: Carrying many an it-bag @RebeccaMinkoff

You know her. You love her. She's the fashion darling behind the 2000s "it-bag," and she's turned her namesake into an empire. She's been on the forefront of contemporary fashion for a decade plus, and she lives, sleeps, and breathes New York.

Her biggest pet peeve? People believing the "overnight success" myth. For her, the notion in our on-demand era that there's an app for success or an elevator to the top is BS. "There's no 'click to buy' here, there's no easy way to cheat this system that I've seen. When you've leveraged everything you own, and you've leveraged future things that you might own, that's kind of the height of 'OK, we're all in on this business.' There is no plan B, so when you don't have a plan B, you just say, 'Fuck it.' I joked the other day to my brother, 'If all else fails, I can go be a receptionist at Dad's doctor's office.' That's plan B. And if you can't risk it, then don't do it."

She keeps herself, her work, and her role in the greater fashion ecosystem in check. A self-awareness gently lines her demeanor, and she's quick to the point: "I think that on the hardest days [fashion] can feel very serious, and trying to remind yourself that we're not curing cancer, we're not fighting a war, we're not providing water and goods to refugees, is important. That helps me put it in perspective."

Perspective and a keen awareness of the fluctuating fashion industry fuel Rebecca's strategic decision making. For her, it's about looking ahead and not getting sidetracked. Her mission is to enable women to lead a more fearless life, not to get caught up with the copycats or the bottomless pit of fast fashion.

"There's always going to be a food chain. Luxury [fashion] is looked at, and then it's diluted. Contemporary has to follow certain trends, and then from there, fast fashion knocks off everything in sight. It's just part of the business. And I could get sucked in trying to be in control and fight lawsuits all day, but I think I've just found that that's a lot of money, and a lot of effort and upset, that you could just use to fuel into keeping yourself going and creative.

"I feel like with the younger millennials and Generation Z, there's this weird idea that because you can like get your Uber in five minutes, and you can get your Prime delivery in a couple of hours, that success should be like that. And I think it's setting people up to fail because then they go, 'I worked so hard for like three months, and nothing happened.' You gotta change the perspective! You gotta work your ass off, and guess what? It's gonna be fucking years and it's going to be nights and it's going to be weekends and it's going to take everything that you've got."

If there's anyone who can attest to late nights and venti coffees, it's Rebecca. She never stops putting her customer first, and she understood very early on the cultural currency of Instagram #OOTDs, bloggers, and brand ambassadors. She, alongside brother and brand cofounder Uri, credits most of their success and innovation to their relationships with and respect for their customers, a.k.a. social-media-savvy, fashion-forward young women. The duo have democratized the brand's New York Fashion Week shows by pioneering a "see now, buy now" approach, which allows their customers to buy the items right from the runway instead of waiting the traditional (and prehistoric) few months that other contemporary lines do to make their runway collections available to the masses.

"Early on, technology enabled us to even exist and to be in touch with our consumer," she says. "We weren't deemed by the editor of a huge magazine or the buyers to be the brand that would be the fashion darling. We really were brought forward by our consumer, and it was only because technology allowed us to do that. I think for us it's always been important to keep that connection. So it's never been technology for technology's sake, it's literally just how do we talk to our customer, and how does she want to be spoken to? So what are those channels that she is on that we can relate to her and have a dialogue with her?"

Consistent dedication, a commitment to connecting with your

consumer, disruptive sales techniques, and a huge lack of plan B. These are just some of the qualities that make Rebecca Minkoff the only Rebecca Minkoff in the game. Check and mate.

Garance Doré on Letting Your Brand Evolve

Name: Garance Doré
Company: Atelier Doré
Name of Her Game: OG Blogger, photographer, illustrator, badass creative director
Most Likely To: Sound chicer than you at any given moment
Find Her: Being aspirational as always at @garancedore

Garance Doré is unapologetically herself. She radiates a cool factor that few could muster up on their best day. Whether she's posting Parisian street style on her blog, sharing work-in-progress illustrations on her Instagram, or partnering with brands under her creative shop, Atelier Doré, she does so in a way that's distinctly Garance.

Her work has a DNA unto itself. Which makes expanding her namesake brand and partnering with global brands . . . tricky. How do you grow your brand and simultaneously maintain control over its evolution? How do you grow a business that is an extension of your own name?

"I think everybody would tell you that my secret weapon is a sense of authenticity," Garance says, "which is a blessing and a curse because when your thing is to be authentic, the choices you make are very important. It can slow you down sometimes, because it's my name on there, and I have to be very conscientious of what I'm doing. But at the end of the day, that's what people respect me for and come to me for."

Her creative-partnership pedigrees speak for themselves. From partnerships with major department stores like Macy's (featuring a video series with none other than the queen herself, Iris Apfel), to makeup brands like NARS, or even retreats with international hotel chains like Mr & Mrs Smith, Garance knows how to stay the course.

"You have to know your goals. If the goal is to, you know, make a lot of money, it's OK, maybe you're going to want to do things a certain way to really please people. If you have more of a voice and an artistic vision, you have to be much more careful about what you do. Everything you do with a brand could change your own brand. There is a lot of co-influence in that." Think back to the chapter on negotiations and the "How Much Do I Show?" Negotiation. The same premise can be applied to the "Which Brand Do I Take Money From?" Negotiation.

For the sake of emphasis and drama, let's repeat that last mantra: "Everything you do with a brand could change your own brand. There is a lot of co-influence in that."

For Garance, it's about understanding her bottom line, having a clear-cut vision of her goals, and letting her ethos guide her decision making.

"You have to ask yourself, what are you looking to do? Some people get into the business of blogging with a very clear idea of becoming a superstar, and with the idea of making a lot of money. Some want to express themselves. Some want to sell product. I think the most important thing is to be very clear. What do you actually want?"

For Garance, she says, "WorkParty is that sense of research. You never really know what's going to make you happy. It's not like, *Once I have that, it's going to be great.* It doesn't work like that. I have this general idea of where I want to go in life and what I want to do, and then I try to explore that through my business."

She goes on, "Does it mean selling in ten years? Or does it mean

having a happy team of people who do creative things, maybe changing the world? I think it's important to play with that, redefine it, and
not be scared to change yourself."

So there it is, life is a happiness project, my friends, and it helps
to be reminded (by creative geniuses) that we're all just here to figure
it out.

Kendra Scott on Failure as Fuel

Name: Kendra Scott
Company: Kendra Scott Designs
Name of Her Game: Jewelry business tycoon
Most Likely To: Be president of the billion-dollar babes' club
Find Her: Sparkling @KendraScott

In 2002, Kendra Scott founded Kendra Scott Designs in her apartment. And while this is a common scene for many businesses' humble
beginnings, Kendra's journey is anything but a common story. The college dropout turned CEO would go on to build a multimillion-dollar
company with thirty-nine retail locations, nearly a thousand employees, and an Austin headquarters that would knock your socks off.

She's the Webster's definition of "optimistic," but don't confuse
her idealism with a smooth, easy path to success. We know by now
that that road doesn't exist.

Remember when I told you to *get ready to fail*? Well, this *Forbes*
one-of-the-richest-self-made-women-in-the-US, failed and failed hard
at her first company, the Hat Box. The CEO is quick to point out her
early failures and how those lessons transcended her business ventures. "The years at the Hat Box gave me a very unique perspective
when I built Kendra Scott. As hard as they were, it was the greatest
gift I have ever been given. Look at failure in those perspectives, that

sometimes you have to go through those things to be able to get you where you're going next in your life. And I look at a lot of those moments of struggle and of hard times as a bridge to get me to where I was going to go and ultimately start Kendra Scott. A lot of people want to glaze over that and talk about the successes and the great things, but it's those elements of your life and the experiences that we go through that really start to weave the fabric of your future together."

Kendra says her best piece of advice for a budding entrepreneur is to "work for someone who is running a great business. I'm always telling students that I meet in schools to intern, intern, intern. Do all aspects of the business. Don't just learn the marketing aspect if you're a marketing major, learn what the production looks like or what the fulfillment looks like or customer service. If you want to own a business, you're going to have to get your hands dirty and really learn all aspects of it."

Resilience required, remember? "I'm a glass-overflowing type of person," Kendra says. "When someone says 'No' or 'That's impossible,' I look for the possibility in impossible. You're going to be told 'No' a lot. Especially when you're a young entrepreneur—you have a new idea, nobody's familiar with you yet. What I always say is that NO's mirror is ON. To me, the conversation is just getting started. So I figure out how I can change this person's perspective. I'm not going to give up, and you're going to continue to hear from me. I'm not a stalker, but I'm definitely not afraid to reengage."

(Now let's repeat that three times, as fast as we can: *Follow up! Follow up! Follow up!*)

"And I keep the conversation going. Nine times out of ten, that 'no' has turned into a 'yes,' and in some cases it's turned into my biggest relationship."

Case closed.

Emily Schuman on Going from Assistant to CEO

Name: Emily Schuman

Company: Cupcakes and Cashmere

Name of Her Game: Going beyond the blog

Most Likely To: Be adding new revenue streams

Find Her: Serving up realness at @byEmily

Nearly ten years ago, Emily Schuman was sneaking into conference rooms and corners at her day job at AOL, taking phone calls with globally recognized brands. Why was she sneaking? They wanted to work with Emily and her blog, not AOL.

Her site is called Cupcakes and Cashmere; it had been a creative outlet and was about to become one of the most influential blogs on the planet.

Fast forward ten years, and now she is running an e-commerce site, has her own fashion line, has published multiple books, and has done brand collaborations with the likes of Coach, a deal she brokered while working her full-time job. And all of that might sound amazing and like a runaway success, but Emily says, "It was actually a slow and gradual progression." Emily admits her media background gave her a leg up in knowing her worth out of the gate, because she had been in ad sales at *Teen Vogue*, *Domino*, and more and knew what the big players were charging and how they were quantifying it. A wise reminder to think of your day job as your investor and, sometimes, your mentor.

Emily says, "I had a good understanding of what I had to offer, I had sizable traffic, analytics on my audience, and when people tried to pay me with eyeshadow and pocket watches, I would say, 'That is a really generous offer, but it doesn't pay the bills and I know my worth.'"

Emily says she worked at both AOL and on her blog for a year and a half before accepting a voluntary layoff package—which she saw as the golden opportunity to transition to full-time blogging. Emily says, "If I was ever going to take it seriously, I would need to dedicate all my time to it." And she did, now running a team of people alongside her husband and business partner, focusing on building the business and "diversifying the brand and never getting comfortable with just one thing."

One of the biggest transitions and learning curves was managing people. "I went from being an assistant in the corporate food chain, the lowest rung, to the CEO," and there were challenges. Emily learned quickly she needed to talk to employees "about setting up expectations from the get-go. I found myself trying to be flexible and carefree but realized so much of my success was driven by the fact that I don't compromise on quality and shouldn't make that exception for the people that work for me."

Emily admits she is hardest on herself and, like most women, suffers from the occasional imposter syndrome, but that is in part why her audience loves her, her authenticity. Her Instagram is not filled with the perfectly styled, coiffed, and magically edited shots of her at New York Fashion Week—more likely, it's her and her kid at the farmers' market. With that, she's making a specific choice: "I open my door into things I love but also things I'm struggling with, like anxiety and my challenges with breastfeeding, and it feels intimidating at first, but then the response is so positive." She goes on, "If I can play a small part in shattering the constant images of perfection in the media we see and make someone feel good about themselves, then that's enough for me. I am after all just a person, too."

Amen.

Christene Barberich on Being the Voice of a Generation

Name: Christene Barberich

Company: Refinery29

Name of Her Game: EIC of a global behemoth

Most Likely To: Be wearing something vintage

Find Her: Creating closet envy at @CRBarberich

"For me, it's all about the voice," says Christene Barberich, whom you may know as cofounder and global editor-in-chief of a little site called Refinery29. A site that truly has become the voice of a millennial female digital-savvy generation, tackling topics from fashion to politics, creating original shows, hosting large-scale experiential art projects like 29Rooms, and generally being the cool kid at the media lunch table that everyone wants to play with. The company is helmed by four cofounders, all of whom, Christene says, "had complementary skills, which really helped with the division of labor and the mix of perspectives."

Christene's skills are in content. She has lived and breathed editorial for as long as she can remember, kicking off her career learning the ropes as an assistant at Condé Nast, a giant company where she was excited to be but oftentimes was servicing an existing way of doing things. It wasn't until she took a job at a small indie publication called *CITY* that she found the courage to "run the show, creating a voice from scratch that really resonated with an audience. So much of what I learned in that role prepared me for starting Refinery29." This newfound confidence was partly due to a supportive boss, who helped hone her brand-building skills. "In the beginning, you keep things tight and focused, in order to get the formula, the balance, the tone, the experience, and really the subtler nuances (that ultimately end up defining the brand) just right. You fly under the radar for a while as you work out the kinks and refine your point of view and scope." A good checklist for any of you looking to start your own brand.

As an editor, she says, "I love that process of finding the story within the story . . . that moment when you realize the author thought the piece was about one thing, but it's about something else altogether, and you're both just totally amazed. I think that also might be a lot like life. You think you're doing or learning one thing, but later on, you realize there was another lesson right behind it. To me, those kinds of moments or experiences link us to one another, make us understand and empathize more fully. That's your job as an editor, to make sure the stories you help to shape really provide a place for the audience to connect and find themselves."

Refinery29 publishes dozens (if not more) of pieces of content daily, has multiple segmented newsletters, and hosts social communities in the millions—all of which Christene oversees. As the company grew and scaled, she knew she needed to take a step back—or, rather, "a step up to see further ahead. It was becoming impossible for me to pivot in and out of stories, from micro to macro, and have the most helpful perspective about how to address the bigger picture—what themes were emerging and what were we collectively standing for as a team?" She brought in talented editors whom she knew would do a great—if not better than she was doing!—job so that she would be able to craft a more cohesive editorial voice versus getting stuck in the weeds.

And while she has truly created & cultivated the career of her dreams, she says, "When things are pretty status quo, I think it's important to find a way to step out of the routine to remind ourselves of who we are in the moment, to feel *happy* and ready for more. Because that makes the work better, and when the work is better, we feel more in alignment with ourselves and what we're really here to do."

The more aligned you feel, the better an entrepreneur you can be.

Morgan DeBaun on Overcoming the Odds

Name: Morgan DeBaun

Company: Blavity

Name of Her Game: Creating community for, by, and with Black millennials

Most Likely To: Make funding more accessible to women

Find Her: Speaking all the truth @MorganDeBaun

Raising investment money is no easy feat. The odds were stacked even higher against Morgan DeBaun, one of just fourteen (four-fucking-teen) Black women to ever secure over $1 million in funding. She's a media maven, a Black community leader, and an all-around inspiration.

And she didn't let the numbers game of it all stand in her way. If anything, the long odds kicked her badassery into overdrive. After landing a job at twenty-two in Silicon Valley, Morgan didn't feel at home in Mountain View or like she had a network of Black creatives, professionals, or advisers she could turn to. So she sought out to create her own movement—building beautiful products and experiences for Black millennials. Which would require funding. And with that mission, she founded Blavity, a company designed to economically and creatively support Black millennials, so they can pursue the work they love and change the world in the process.

"I didn't go to MIT, I didn't go to Stanford, and my family isn't necessarily full of entrepreneurs," Morgan says. "So I think there was a huge learning curve in terms of even just the vocabulary, when you're going to the table, and the finance parts, the ramifications of different terms, and investors, and so it was really intimidating raising [money] for the first time. And even now, four years in, it almost never ends. Every single level I'm finding that I have to learn new things, and perhaps for non-women or non–people of color, there's more of a network where you can get access to information. You can call your friends who have done this before. Or your advisers. Or family—your dad, your mom—who have already done this.

"But for women, or for people of color, we may not have anyone to call. So I think we're spending a lot more time, and I think I spent a lot of time, researching. Until, I would say, the last six months or nine months, I finally have a network of advisers and people around me who I can call and be like, 'What the heck does this mean? What is preferred stock, what is this? How is this going to impact me and the business as we continue to grow?' That was the biggest barrier, I think, and then once you're up and running, and you get your first money—the first money's always the hardest—and then you're like, 'Oh, I got this.' But the first check, network, and vocabulary. Those have been the largest hurdles."

Since founding Blavity in 2014, Morgan is straight killing the game. She and her three cofounders have acquired additional companies, hoping to scale their media empire and conference series, EmpowerHer, in the next year.

But even with large-scale growth and industry accolades, when you're the only woman in the room, imposter syndrome can creep in uninvited. This feeling is magnified when the numbers are so specifically stacked against women of color.

"I have three cofounders who are all men, so I could not put them in the room when I was trying to raise money," she says. "If I did, the investors would have just defaulted to them, and it's mine, right? So I couldn't afford to do that. So I actually, recently, had to have a conversation with them because we're getting into a stage where Blavity's getting really big, and so our fundraising asks and the evaluation of the company's getting large, and the investors can change and become very institutional. And very corporate. And very male. And very white.

And I had a bit of insecurity because I felt like, 'Am I doing the company a disservice? Am I going to get worse terms for us as a company because I'm a woman and I am Black? Would it actually be better if one of our other cofounders raised for us because they're going to be able to negotiate better terms because they're men?' So we had to have this whole philosophical conversation, and ultimately I'm still doing it and it's still me, but those are weird trade-offs to think about."

And nevertheless, she persisted. And while this year she has officially moved out of her apartment that shared a wall with Blavity's Los Angeles office, she's still in a committed relationship with the business she's built. She never forgets her mission, and she's always looking for transactional ways to put money back into her community. "People think there has to be such a grand scale, and it doesn't. It really makes a difference if you say, 'We're spending $55,000 this month on vendors. Can I put $55,000 back into the Black community?'"

Hindsight is always 20/20, though. If you're conditioned to believe your options are scarce, or your dreams are too big, what does that do to your ambition?

"I wish I'd had a sense that 'you are enough.' When I first started, I was like, 'I'm going to get these cofounders and get these things and people because I'm not enough!' And I am grateful that I have my cofounders, grateful that I went through the journey that I did, but I do wonder, though, if I hadn't been told so much that it wasn't possible, and I hadn't listened to those people as much, how much further I'd be? Even though I know I've done well in my short period of time, what if I had those six months back when I was spinning in a circle?"

Hear that, ladies? Let's reclaim our time and keep that spinning to a minimum because we are enough. You. Are. Enough.

chapter twelve

Work Hard, Party On

OH MY GOSH. You've made it. You've made it through the work. The chapters on hiring and firing. Understanding your brand and personal equity. Reliving the hardest parts of my career and life journey with me. Thanks for sticking in there with the work, because guess what?

Now it's time for the party.

You've heard from me. You've heard from the women I admire. And now it's your turn.

WorkParty is a new approach to work for a new generation of women. We're here to inspire the next gen of CEOs and bosses who can make all the change we've been talking about real. And we can do it on our own terms and have some fun in the process. This is Work-Party. But how?

You don't have to be in Los Angeles or New York. What you need to do is build community with the women in your city, in your internet sphere, and IRL. Take your side hustle seriously, call yourself an entrepreneur, and build up your girl gang so much that they can't ignore you.

And always, always, always reference the WorkParty 10 Career Commandments.

1. Start by Starting

Don't wait for a community to find you. We are in a niche-as-fuck era. There are fandoms everywhere, networks everywhere, and ways to build your tribe. Start a group on Facebook! Publish an essay online! Set up a website to sell your art! Whatever your passion or discipline is, get after it. If you've had a business idea, make time for it. Make a plan. Break down big to-dos into little, achievable tasks. There's no time like the present to start by starting, take the leap, and file the LLC.

If you're feeling stuck or unsure about your career, focus on finding your community and let opportunity find you. Truthfully, one of the best things I've done to build my tribe and meet business BFFs is join a book club! Maybe you are going to start a WorkParty book club—I know the first title you could read.

2. Be a Fucking Pleasure to Work With

Self-explanatory, but worth reiterating. Real life is not how Hollywood portrays it, and the Miranda Priestlys or Ari Golds of the silver screen are not to be idolized or revered.

There isn't any magic way through this one. On your worst day, be a fucking pleasure to work with. On your best day, be a fucking pleasure to work with. It's the only way we all get through this wild ride and come out with glowing recommendations on the other side.

3. Bring in the Experts

That's right. There is no f-ing way you're doing this alone, so bring in the experts when you don't know how to do something yourself—as I like to say, staff your weakness. Bring in people who are smarter and

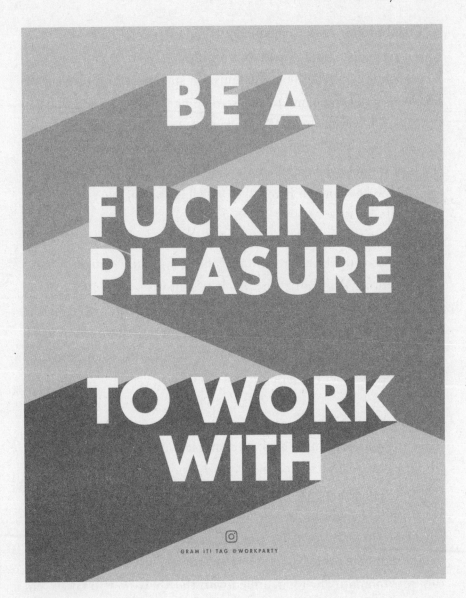

better than you. People who know and understand sides of your business that you don't. That means legal. That means accounting. The people who can handle the parts of biz that you don't (yet) understand. This also falls in line with taking your business, no matter how big or small, seriously.

4. Collaboration over Competition

This is one of the most important missions of Create & Cultivate: collaboration over competition. That mission statement runs through the lifeblood of the company. And it's something that the women who join us onstage know all about. It's also our most re-'Grammed image coming out of our NYC conference, proving that even beyond the thousands of women who gathered, thousands more wanted to share it.

No one has time for haters. We are all in this together.

5. Don't Let the Bastards Get You Down

We're done with "locker room talk" and "boys' club" antics. When I started writing *WorkParty*, I had male executives saying, "Why would I take business advice from a book that has frilly handwriting on the cover and pink poufy shoes?" They don't get it, and we need to teach by showing, not telling. Build your business, make the money, get the power, and don't let the bastards get you down.

6. Know Your Shit

Invest in your continued education and learning. That can be literal (there are so. many. free. online. courses.) or metaphorical—but your brain is your value. Marketplaces are changing and changing fast. Don't get so caught up in your ego or craft that you think you don't have more to learn, because you always, always do. Invest time and energy into being the expert you (1) claim you are and (2) know you can be. Walk into any room armed with the know-how to knock 'em dead.

7. Money Is Power

Capitalism is our reality, and feminism is the name of our game. If we're going to effect change and rise to the top, we need to control the dollars. This begins with reinvesting those dollars in each other.

Where and how you can, hire women, recommend women, and invest in women. Bottom line, bottom dollar, it matters.

8. Find Your Tribe

Humans are built for interaction with other humans. We do not thrive in isolation! Remember this. Seek out connection! Find your tribe, and get specific about who you surround yourself with. And remember that sometimes you need to humanize and empathize with people you don't necessarily like. Offer connection to receive connection, and bring your authentic self to your search.

9. Resiliency Required

No one said it would be easy, so find your formula for resiliency. For some it's meditation, for some it's cardio, for some it's therapy. Or it's a mix of all of that. Or some of that. Everyone has their tactics for dealing with the shoulder-crushing pressures of their careers! I recommend a dog! Find your own tactics—you are going to need them.

10. Pay It Forward

Never forget: One email, one recommendation, one meeting can change the trajectory of one woman's life. You have to put your work out there, but you also need to put it out there for other women. Because that woman will pay it forward, and then another woman will, and then so on and so forth.

We can all do this. So let's do it.

Work hard.

Party on.

glossary

1099 tax form: The IRS paperwork freelancers typically have to fill out.

angel investor: An affluent individual who provides capital for a business startup, usually in exchange for convertible debt or ownership equity.

brand: A name, term, design, symbol, or other feature that distinguishes an organization or product from its rivals in the eyes of the customer.

business model: How your company makes money, whether through commerce or product business or service business.

capital: Money, dollar bills, and often the investment you use to build a business.

cause: Bad behavior that creates the conditions to be fired or to fire.

commission: Typically a percentage of sales you own or win.

company culture: The general vibes and ethos of a company.

corner-office goals: Top-level executive offices are typically in the corner with a good view. That's the dream.

crowdsource: Using your social community to source money, ideas, or information.

curation: Collecting and sorting information in an artful or calculated way.

disrupt, or disruption: A company that creates new market conditions in an old industry (e.g., Uber to the taxi industry or Casper to the mattress industry).

equity: The value of shares of a company and percentage ownership of company.

fiduciary duties: Responsibilities appointed to parties who hold legal or ethical relationships of trust, also typically in relationship to that person handling financial matters.

first to market: Being the first company to present a product or idea to the masses.

force majeure: Unforeseeable circumstances that prevent someone from fulfilling a contract.

forensic accountant: Accountants specifically trained to search for evidence of mishandled or misappropriated money.

influencer: Most generally a person with influence over other people, but modernly a person with a substantial social media following.

intellectual property: A work or invention that is the result of creativity, such as a manuscript or a design, to which one has rights and for which one may apply for a patent, copyright, trademark, etc.

iterate: To repeat and change.

KPI: Key performance indicator, a.k.a. what results matter most to you.

LLC: A limited liability company is the United States–specific form of a private limited company. It is a business structure that combines the pass-through taxation of a partnership or sole proprietorship with the limited liability of a corporation.

noncompete clause: Part of the agreement under which one party (usually an employee) agrees not to enter into or start a similar profession or trade in competition against another party (usually that of the employer).

operating agreement: A legal document that outlines the ownership and member duties of your limited liability company. This agreement allows you to set out the financial and working relations among business owners and between members and managers.

ownership stakes: The percentage of stock each owner or manager in the company holds.

phantom equity: A contractual agreement between a corporation and recipients that bestows upon the grantee the right to a cash payment at a designated time or in association with a designated event in the future (like a buyout).

recession: A business cycle contraction that results in a general slowdown in economic activity (a.k.a. not good).

ROI: Return on investment. For instance, if I am spending (investing) five dollars on Facebook marketing, in return I want to see ten dollars in sales on my site, so my ROI is five dollars.

sales or pitch deck: The sales material you present to prospective clients that outlines your vision and specifics.

scale: The characteristic of a business that describes its capability to cope and perform under an increased or expanding workload. A business that scales well will be able to maintain or even increase its level of performance or efficiency when tested by larger operational demands.

scope creep: When clients ask you to do work outside of the agreed-upon and contracted services.

stock swap: Acquisition of a company in which payment consists of stock in the buying company.

swag: Easily confused with "swagger," but rather free stuff (think totes, notebooks, and, in my case, makeup and fashion items).

venture capital: A type of private equity, a form of financing that is provided by firms or funds to small, early-stage, emerging firms that are deemed to have high growth potential, or which have demonstrated high growth.

vertical: A category of industry or market used as an organizational tool.

whitespace: Where unmet and unarticulated needs are uncovered to create innovation opportunities.

boss gloss

The baddest bosses in the game. Follow along and support their journeys.

Hillary Kerr | @hillarykerr

Katherine Power | @KatherinePower

Jeni Britton Bauer | @Jenisplendid

Ellen Bennett | @hedleyandbennett

Issa Rae | @IssaRae

Mandy Moore | @mandymooremm

Brooklyn Decker | @BrooklynDecker

Kristen Vang | @kvang

Alisa Leonard | @little_altars

Alex LoCasto | @TheFashionBrief

Raina Penchansky | @rp1313

Jen Gotch | @jengotch

Alli Webb | @AlliWebb

Jen Rubio | @jennifer

Jihan Zencirli | @geronimo

Michelle Lee | @heymichellelee @allure

Aimee Song | @aimeesong

Rebecca Minkoff | @RebeccaMinkoff

Garance Doré | @garancedore

Kendra Scott | @KendraScott

Emily Schuman | @emilyschuman

Christene Barberich | @CRBarberich

Morgan DeBaun | @MorganDeBaun

Sarah Kunst | @sarahkunst

Daina Trout | @DainaTrout

Ruthie Lindsey | @ruthielindsey

acknowledgments

To every woman who has ever sent an email on my behalf or given me that extra leg up to get me in the door, and to those of you who have supported me emotionally and even physically throughout my life and career, thank you. And thanks especially to Diana Ventimiglia, without whom this book would not be possible. And to my publisher, Jennifer Bergstrom, and fabulous editor, Kate Dresser.

To my sister, Jessica, who, no matter what time of day, will take my call and let me be insecure, sad, happy, angry, and very much myself and never judge me for it. Who flew across the country to pick up the pieces of my life and help me put them back together. I love you always, Jess #collegegirls.

To my squad of ladies who have been my support system and cheerleaders: Delia Tethong, Joanna Pawlowska, Angeline Vuong, Courtney Bensik, Rachel Mae Furman, Jeanine Pesce, Daniele Piersons, Vang, Alisa Leonard, Whitney Leigh Morris, and Jane Helpern. Your unending support, passion, and ability to tell me to get the hell off my phone and have a glass of wine is beyond appreciated; I love you ladies more than you will know.

For Raina, Reesa, Sherry, and Allison, the best partners a girl could ask for, thank you for always supporting my vision and believing in me.

To Aunt Deb, for constantly inspiring me to reach for more than what is right in front of me.

And my dad, Gene, whose work ethic till this day is awe-inspiring, who, despite my going to a college with no football team, rooted for me day in and day out to succeed. Your support is the best gift I could ask for, and I could never repay you for everything you have done.

To Noah Wiley, who is always excited to see me when I walk in the door no matter what type of mood I am in, your snuggles are unprecedented.

And to the C&C dream team, our group texts give me life, and so does your beautiful ambition and hard work. I love you, ladies!

And to David, a.k.a. Mr. Johnson, a.k.a. my better half. I love you so much and feel so lucky to have you as my partner. You are the Yang to my Yin, my constant gut check and calming presence, my best friend and the love of my life.

For JoAnn, a.k.a. Clover, this is for you. You have worked your whole life to give Jess and me every opportunity, and I am forever grateful.